1.10 18

Henri Wasselaar

Facing a German Firing Squad in Twelve Hours

Dr. Henri Wetselaar's Biography

By
Dr. Henri Wetselaar

Facing A German Firing Squad
In 12 Hours
All Rights Reserved
© 2014
by
Dr. Henri Wetselaar
ISBN: 978-1-934051-71-9

Editor: Denice Whitmore
Interior Design: Jo Wilkins
Cover Art: Maxwell Alexandar Drake
Graphics Placement: Audrey Balzart

Published in the United States of America
using enviromentally friendly materials,
in cooperation with:

Mystic Publishers
www.mysticpublishers.com

I dedicate this book to my parents
to whom I owe so much.

With love to my children:
Henri Jr., Janina, Misty and Jack
They are so special.

Facing a German
Firing Squad
in Twelve Hours

CHAPTER I
My Early Years

My family had a lot of history and memories of Indonesia, a large Pacific Ocean country, run as a colony by the Netherlands for over 300 years. That came from both of my parents, all four grandparents and our great grandparents. My mother, in fact, when speaking Dutch had a slight Indonesian accent. Many Dutch professionals and military personnel were sent to Indonesia over the centuries and spent a certain number of years serving overseas until they retired back home to The Netherlands.

My father's father (born in 1870) was assigned to a military base on mid-Java in the town of Magelang where he functioned as captain-pharmacist for the KNIL (the Royal Dutch Indonesian Army). Magelang was a small town, located very close to one of the largest Buddhist temples in the world. I don't know how he and my grandmother tolerated the heat. I don't believe they had air conditioning in the late 1800's.

My father was born in Magelang in 1895. Four years later, twin brothers joined him. I called them

Oom Gé (Uncle Gé) and Oom Max. The whole family moved back to Holland when the boys were still relatively young.

My mother was born in Djoeana on North Central Java, some two hundred miles north of my father's birthplace. 'Opa Wit' (my grandfather) worked as a school principal. He later played a big role in my life.

We often ate Indonesian food at home, especially when we had a family gathering with grandparents, uncles and aunts. Our cooks at home had been taught to cook the Oriental dishes, the most famous ones being "rijsttafel" (Dutch for rice table), nasi goring, or bami goreng (fried rice or fried noodles). I really miss those dishes. Some of us loved the Indonesian hot spices, such as sambal, which was very hot. I remember my Oom Max perspiring after such a meal.

Opa Wit told me about a time when he worked as a teacher on the Island of Sumatra, and in particular in the most northern province of Atjeh. He got along with the people very well but Atjeh had a fanatical, radical section of the population, which was fiercely independent and wanted 'freedom from the white oppressors'.

One time in Northern Sumatra, a group of white people traveled on a country road when a group of radicals spotted them. They tied the whites to trees on each side of the road and brutally murdered them. The details of the slaughter were told to me but are too gruesome to print in this book.

I was born in the city of Breda, in the South of the Netherlands in 1924, about five miles from the Belgian border and three or four miles from the village where

Vincent Van Gogh was born. About fifty thousand people lived in Breda. It was an historic city dating back to around the 1100's. It had a large castle in the middle of the city, surrounded by water, close to the center of the city.

My parents were both dentists and had degrees from the University of Utrecht, a city located in the center of The Netherlands. Oom Gé had a Ph. D. as a Pharmacist and lived in our hometown. Oom Max lived some 4-5 hours away from us by train.

We were always excited to spend of couple of weeks of our summer vacations with Oom Max and his wife, Tante Iet. Oom Max was a champion tennis player in Holland and competed at Wimbledon. Sometimes I would meet a stranger and when I mentioned my last name, they would ask if I was related to Max Wetselaar. This made me very proud.

When Oom Max got older, he took up golf and became an international champion golfer. We were excited when we heard that he had played with the Kings of Belgium and Sweden.

I must confess that we, as children, were very impressed with Oom Max. We should have admired my own father as much and should have told him so. A hardworking dentist, his first thought was always to look after his family. Thanks to him, we had a good life and were given a good upbringing.

We always bragged about Oom Max after we returned home from our summer vacation. Of course, Oom Max was special to us. I remember he took us with him to watch his tennis match or when he went to practice. Later on, the same happened on the golf course. I will never forget the tip he gave. "When your ball lands just off the green in the first cut, take your six iron to pitch it towards the cup." I never played golf in Europe but took it up in Canada after I immigrated there in 1954.

When I was a child the KMA (Royal Military Academy) was located in a castle near the center of the city, where young Dutch officers were schooled and trained by the Dutch military. The young cadets used to come to my parents' dental office, which was not far away. When our family got bigger and my mother had four children, she gradually stopped practicing and my father looked after the young officers. He always told us that they were very pleasant patients.

My father's and mother's practice was located only about five hundred yards from the center of our old city. The center consisted of a plaza with old cobblestones. City Hall was located on that plaza and right across sat the old church, a tall historic building. Next to the church was Beker & Wetselaar, my grandfather's pharmacy, which my granddad ran with his friend Mr. Beker. I remember visiting the pharmacy and watching the technicians carefully folding pieces of paper containing medication in powder form. There were no tablets and capsules as we have now.

City Hall was (and still is now) an architecturally beautiful building and it housed a museum with beautiful paintings. We went there for birth certificates and such. After my grandfather retired in the late 30's his son, my uncle Oom Gé, took over and lived with his family above the store.

4

Our city was a good place to live. Most people were decent and hard working. In Southern Holland, Catholic was the most popular religion, in contrast to the northern two-thirds of the country who were mostly Protestants. In our family, religion played practically no role although my father was baptized in the Wallonian (Protestant) church. We belonged to a very large group of people in the Netherlands whose fathers and grandfathers were churchgoers but who had drifted away from that. The 10 commandments still ruled the lives and actions of these people, as was the case in our family.

Our city was peaceful. I cannot remember any public violence or demonstration. I'm sure that occasionally a crime took place but I just don't remember hearing of it. Our safety in general was very much better than in Las Vegas, where I am living now. Small children rode their bikes to school, which is somewhat risky in our modern world. Our schools were not far from our home, so we went home for lunch and then back to school.

Our education and teachers were of high quality, and political correctness did not yet exist. I was privileged to go to a top high school (there was no such animal as "middle school", we had 6 years of primary school and then went to high school for 6 years). We learned six languages--Dutch, French, English, German, classical Latin and Greek. We had courses in math, including algebra, trigonometry and even some higher math in grades fifth and sixth. We also learned history, geography, physics, chemistry and biology. When I came to Canada as a young physician I was told by an educational authority that my high school diploma from Holland was just about equivalent to a North American college degree. In the Netherlands we have no colleges. After high school we enter university.

Sports were as big in Holland as elsewhere. Soccer was popular. As for my friends and myself we played grass hockey on the weekends. The Netherlands has a good international name in grass hockey and our team usually performs well in the Olympics, often ending up in the top three. It is not too violent, although I got hit by a ball on the right side of my face and had to be taken to the hospital for sutures. I still have a slight scar. If we didn't play hockey we would go swimming with friends on the weekends in a nearby lake or river or we would go to the forest, which was very close to our city, to play or to pick blueberries.

Every summer during our vacation my mother took us to the North Sea where she rented a small house for about 3 weeks. The village were we stayed was Zoutelande in the province of Zeeland. We played on the beach, swam in the North Sea, built sand castles and rode on rental horses. My grandparents, aunts, uncles and cousins would often join us. What unforgettable, wonderful memories I have of those summers.

One time we stayed in a rental house about 300 yards from the dunes and the sea. We saw a huge silver cigar sliding by us in the sky, from the east over the dunes, gradually disappearing over the westward sea. It was 1937 and this was the famous Zeppelin called the Hindenburg coming from Germany on its way to New York, where it would burst into flames upon arrival and many people would lose their lives. What a magnificent site to see this big monster moving in the sky without making any sound.

Another unforgettable occurrence happened when I went with a few other kids to the little harbor about four in the morning. We boarded a Dutch fishing boat and travelled with them for most of the day in the North Sea watching the men fish for shrimp and fish with huge nets. We came home feeling very important and excited to tell our stories about travelling on the big sea.

Once, while swimming in the ocean, a baby dolphin who had lost his mother and family came up to me and cuddled itself to my chest. I instantly fell in love with the little animal and treated it like my own baby. He wouldn't let go so we went to shore on the sand, where our little friend became an instant sensation with the people on the beach. We didn't know what to do. Some caretakers of the nearest zoo came and took care of him. I never found out where he ended up.

I wandered along the ocean when we came upon a small group of young people playing baseball, which in Holland was a rare sport. Some of the players had recently been to America and wanted to introduce baseball to their Dutch friends. The players asked me to join them. They explained the game to me and I enthusiastically accepted their invitation, starting 'at bat'.

When the pitcher threw the first pitch I hit a big home run. You can imagine how excited and impressed everyone was and I became a "hero." For the rest of the afternoon I was a first pick when teams were put together but I never excelled again. The brief moment of fame lingered for some time and boosted my morale. I don't believe I ever played baseball again.

Looking back, I am amazed what a very different world we lived in before the war. We felt so safe, stable and secure compared to our present world. In our early, mid and late teens, my younger brother and I would say goodbye to my mother and go on our bicycles with our friends. We would go to the forest or the lake for the day with a few sandwiches. We just had to be home in time for dinner. In our present world that would be unthinkable, especially in Las Vegas where I live.

I must admit however that we always got one warning from my mother, "When you go deep inside the forest, stay together, because there could be a man who hurts children when they are alone."

One time my friend Theo Vander Loos invited me to go hiking for a few days and lo and behold, my mother let me go. We walked with our backpacks along the main road to the next city, which was Tilburg. It was a distance of about 14 miles. We only had a few guilders on us. We stayed at a farm in the hayshed for free and intended to keep doing this in the next few days, offering to do some work for the farmer. I am ashamed to say that I chickened out after the first night and went home.

Theo bravely went on further East on his way to Eindhoven, which was a city somewhat larger than

Breda. Eindhoven is the home of the world-renowned Philips factory, which produces light bulbs, TV sets and other electronics. Many Americans look at their Philips TV every day.

Our family would occasionally take a Sunday bicycle trip to Belgium with family or friends. It was only a few miles to the South and we would have a nice lunch or dinner in a Belgian restaurant. The people in Northern Belgium speak Flemish, which is so close to Dutch that we can understand each other (in Southern Belgium people speak French).

My grandfather, Opa Wit died in the late 30's and we were living in his house (my mother probably inherited it). It was adjacent to a large grassy field and I have wonderful memories of living there and playing with friends in the neighborhood.

My father took us to a special store to buy some wooden slats, large sheets of colored paper and a big roll of string. At home he built a large kite with a long tail. We would then go to the big field and fly this six-foot tall kite, competing with others kite fliers. We sometimes had competitions to see who could fly the highest. Some people bought special string, which had been imbued with fine glass. Their trick was to cross their string with yours and make a sawing movement, which would then cut your string causing your kite to fly away. Although this actually happened I must say it was very rare and severely condemned.

We lived a wonderful life. Our blissful existence did not prepare us for the changes about to happen in the world.

My View of History

Indonesia is a huge country and is an archipelago north of Australia. Indonesia had been a colony of the Netherlands since the 1600's.

A few words about colonies in general. Many people in the west believe that European colonies in Asia and Africa were centers of cruel oppression and greed, where the occupiers took all the oil and minerals home and became filthy rich. Members of my family going back to the 1700's were colonialists. In Jakarta (in colonial times named Batavia) there was a street named General Wetselaar Street, named after one of my forefathers. I'm sure this street is now renamed. Our forefathers were actually very good stewards in the colonies and were motivated to run the colonies well. Indonesia enjoyed the best known healthcare in the world and also the best education. I know, because my grandfather (Opa Wit) helped me with my homework and taught me a lot after he pensioned out and returned to the Netherlands.

In early 1942, not long after the Pearl Harbor's disaster, Indonesia was attacked by the Japanese. The Dutch Army, Navy and Air Force fought bravely side by side with the British forces but were defeated by the Japanese. When Japan had conquered the whole of Indonesia, the Dutch together with some other people were put in Japanese concentration camps, mainly on Java. The cruelty of the occupiers was notorious and several prisoners were beheaded.

Interestingly one can say a good word here for the Japanese: The beheading was swift and done by one slash of a sword. The modern radical Islamist sits those prisoners in front of him. The beheader then takes a knife and while grabbing the prisoner's hair, begins slowly and deliberately to cut his victim's throat. Compared to that the Japanese were civilized.

The prevailing opinion is that colonialism was evil and unjust. I recently asked a man from Pakistan "were you better or worse off under the British than now, being independent?"

He said, "We were much better off under the British."

Obviously "independence" is theoretically better. This is just some food for thought.

After World War II, several Indonesian students came to Holland to study at the Dutch Universities. Some of these young men came in groups to our home, especially to eat their native foods. They became good friends. Many of them later went back to Indonesia in the late 1940's and early '50's when Indonesia gained full independence from the Netherlands and played important roles in high offices in the new Indonesian government.

As many readers will remember a few years ago a huge tsunami hit the Eastern part of the Indian Ocean. Thousands died from the huge waves and Atjeh was hit particularly hard.

*My mother (about 6) with her little brother
in Indonesia (town of Djoeana, Western Java)
in front of her parent's home.*

Typical Dutch scenery.

Military gathering in Breda in World War I.

My father (Henri Wetselaar Sr.) as second lieutenant, being mobilized in World War I.

*My father (front center) with his friends
during the mobilization in 1914.*

*My father (2nd front left) during the mobilization
of the Netherlands (1914-16) in World War I
at the Dutch-German border.*

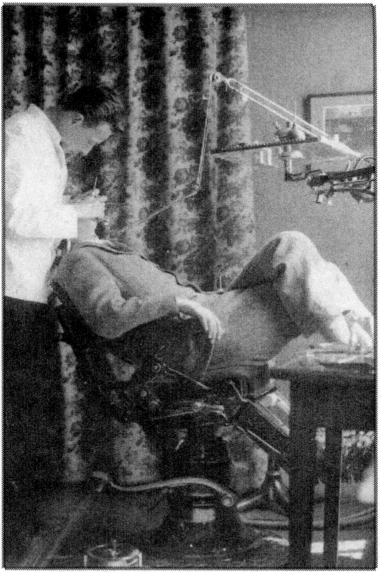

Henri Wetselaar Sr. practicing dentistry in the 1920's.

Breda 1960. The city's central plaza my granfather's pharmacy was in the far right in front of the church.

*Myself as a baby with my father,
grandfather and great-grandfather.*

The writer about age 5.

The Wetselaar family with Opa Wit
(my mother's father in 1937).

The brothers Wetselaar as boy scouts, about 1936.

Four generations, my son Henri Jr. sits on my lap. 1947

CHAPTER II
May 10 1940 Beginning of WWII
German Invasion of the Netherlands

Our wonderful world of peace, happiness and harmony was brutally broken on the tenth of May 1940. The Germans crossed our borders about fifty miles to our east with their finest, most modern military apparatus: heavy tanks, motorized vehicles and motorcycles with German Messerschmit's and Stuka bombers flying overhead. Our Dutch military put up a brave but short resistance. At the same time, the Germans crossed into Belgium, Northern France, Denmark and Norway. This was the start of World War II for us.

Officially, war had been declared in September 1939. The German Army invaded Poland in collusion with the Russians, who invaded Poland from the East. Poor Poland had been under Russian occupation for one hundred years when finally in World War I the Great Polish Marshall Pilsudski liberated his country. Therefore, Poland had been a free country for only about twenty years.

We heard about the German invasion and word

spread around town like wild fire. We were all scared. Our poor parents were far more worried and uncertain about the situation than us children, for whom adventures are somewhat exciting. The day after the German invasion, the mayor of Breda ordered the total citizenry of the city to evacuate to the southwest. It has never been clear what the reasoning was for this decision. Was it because we would be caught in the fighting or fear that the German Army would brutalize us? We will never know precisely. Only a few people of our city had cars or trucks. My parents packed as much as they could in backpacks. We got on our bicycles, my father with my little sister, who was then seven on a little seat on a bar in front of him, then my mother, my oldest sister who was almost eighteen, myself, sixteen and my youngest brother, fifteen. My father took as much as he could get together. On we went on a packed road with thousands of others going south into Belgium.

I will never know what my parents must have gone through emotionally. There was panic and chaos on the road on which thousands travelled. The first night, my father managed to convince a farmer to let us sleep in his barn on the hay. The next day we were getting close to Antwerp, which is on a large body of water. We saw a few military motorcycles from the French Army but they were not very impressive. Not long after, we saw the first enemy troops, in large armed vehicles and tanks looking threatening and determined. They basically left the civilians alone.

My father decided to cross the large river just south of Antwerp and managed to rent a small rowboat in which we packed bicycles and all to cross. God knows what would have happened if the boat had capsized? On the west side of the water we got back on our bicycles and travelled westward and then North which brought us back in to our own country in the province of Zeeland , where we had spent our summer vacations. We stayed in the South of Zeeland and were not able to go to our favored island.

That night we reached a large farm, and again my father managed to make a deal with the farmer who put us up in a large barn. The farmer and his family treated us very well and we stayed there for about ten days. In that time the general situation in Holland had simmered down. Our Military had capitulated and the country was now fully occupied by the Germans.

In the area where we were, there was relatively little fighting. On the first day of the invasion, the German Luftwaffe's Stuka bombers had bombed the city of Rotterdam, an important international harbor city. The structural damage was enormous and thousands of Dutch were killed. Rotterdam is only thirty miles north of our home city Breda.

After about twelve days, my father decided that we should try and go home. So we all climbed on our bikes and set off for Breda. Our travel was relatively uneventful. We did see thousands of German soldiers, armored cars and tanks along the road. We reached Breda in three days traveling through northern Belgium. Our home remained intact and orderly. What a "civilized" world (apart from the war), we were living in now that I think back to it.

The homes in Breda were unchanged. Imagine, in the world we live now, making a total population leave their homes and belongings, and then coming back two weeks later. Many homes would have been vandalized.

Now we entered a brand new chapter of our lives. We lived in a country, occupied by a military enemy. What changes did we notice? The local newspapers now only presented pro German and anti-allies news. It was hard to know what the military situation was in the rest of Europe.

North Africa was also an important battleground. At first, the famous German Marshall Rommel made progress against the British and U.S. troops, driving them eastward into Egypt. Later on, the British Generals Alexander and Montgomery turned things around and began to defeat and push the German troops back into Tobruk and further into Libya.

We followed these movements anxiously, hoping for our eventual liberation in the future not knowing when it would come. How did we get our information? By radio. Officially, radios were forbidden by the occupiers. The people whose homes were searched by the Germans were punished if radios were found. We had a couple of small radios, which we hid carefully. Every day we spent some time listening to the BBC from London and we were so excited when we heard of any progress made by the British-American military anywhere in the world. A speech by Churchill was always the highlight.

After December 1941, when Pearl Harbor was attacked, the world situation became even more alarming and interesting. We listened to the radio whenever we could.

Life in general moved along quite normal from 1940-1945 but we lived under constant threat. In the early part of the occupation, we were shocked when our local newspaper published the names of twenty-five local, prominent, well-known citizens, who had all been arrested for no reason and executed by firing squad. The Germans did this to put the scare of death in all of us so that we wouldn't commit any acts of sabotage.

We went to school as before. We even went to class to learn German from our German teacher. My father went every morning on his bicycle across town to his dental practice.

I was 16 years old and my friends and I were outraged at the foreign occupation of our country. So I joined the Dutch Underground Army or resistance force, which looked for ways to sabotage the occupiers. Unfortunately, we could not do much without weapons.

The Dutch Underground Army's main functions were to gather information about enemy forces and transmit it by radio to a source in England.

We knew each other only by first name and secrecy was the highest requirement in our activities. We operated in groups no larger than four or five people and only one of us knew one other person in another group. We possessed only one rifle in my group and occasionally would take it (carefully wrapped up) into the deepest part of the forest to practice with it. This was all very risky business, because any apprehension by the Germans would have meant immediate execution.

My parents knew that we were involved in the underground but they never talked about it. They knew it was risky but never asked us to stop. I believe in their hearts they were proud of us.

My father's dental office took up the ground floor of his building. Our family used to live in the upper three floors but in the mid to late thirties, we moved to a much smaller, nice little house towards the outskirts of our city. This house sat by a small city park and lake. During that period, the top three floors above the practice were rented out. After the German occupation of our city in May 1940, my father was forced to rent the three uppers floors to the German military administration.

In midsummer 1940, I rode my bike downtown and happened to pass by my father's practice. I saw a huge German Hakenkreuz-Nazi flag hanging out the second floor window waving right over my father's practice. This insulted and angered me. I parked my bike and entered the first floor of the building through a small side door. I went upstairs. There was nobody around and I proceeded to the first floor's front window. I opened the window and reached for the flagpole, trying to untie the knots in the rope that attached the flag. I was not strong enough to untie the knots, they were too tight. I kept trying but had to give up and left the building.

My presence in the building and my attempt to sabotage had not gone unnoticed. Within a few hours, I was arrested by the German "Green Police" and taken to the old city castle where the German military headquarters were located. I was not handled very nicely and put in a cell.

This was not the first time that I was in this castle. At age two, I was chosen to be a "brides boy" in a sketch which would be presented on stage by the Dutch Cadets. I was part of an on-stage fictional wedding at their yearly celebration. Although I was very little, I remember the cadets were very happy with my get-up.

This time was different. I was locked up and jailed in a small, cold room. I received a small meal. A couple of times I was harshly interrogated and it was clear to me that I'd committed a serious act. I had insulted the German flag and would receive the same punishment as all saboteurs' — execution by firing squad the next morning. I was terrified and shook like a leaf.

Our home was only a fifteen-minute walk from the castle. My parents were mortified when they found out I had been arrested. My father walked down to the castle to face the German Commander. My father had treated a few of the officers in his dental practice. He reminded the Commander that he was leasing the upper floors of his practice to some of the German staff (by force, of course).

That evening he begged and pleaded for a long time so that they finally changed their decision. The fact that I looked around thirteen of fourteen, had a thin build, pale complexion and owly looking glasses also helped some.

I received a very stern lecture about how to respect

27

the German flag and we left to go home, shaking in our shoes. There, we held a small celebration with the whole family. I believe that my parents were proud of me but they never expressed it. Neither did they tell me to avoid the Dutch Underground Forces.

For a short time, I had been one of the youngest German prisoners of war in World War II. As a child, I did not quite fully appreciate what had happened. However, one can only imagine what my poor parents went through.

The war went on during the early 40's. My brother, my sister and I continued to go to high school and to do as well as we could. Food was harder to come by compared with pre war times. We had food stamps from the government. Sometimes my father went with us on a Sunday on our bikes out of town to the local farmers to buy some extra food.

The Underground sometimes gave me far more aggressive and dangerous assignments. In 1942, I was asked to bring a large block of dynamite out of town to a certain farm located not far from a railroad track. I carefully packed the dynamite and placed it over the back frame of my bicycle.

I followed their directions to a certain country road. I would recognize the farm by a red pickup truck parked on the right side of the road between two trees, with the license plate number provided, sitting in front of the farmhouse. I went on my journey and travelled some fifteen to twenty miles until I found my destination. The courage of teenager's is hard to measure. The risk of being caught on the road was not so small. I passed and encountered vehicles some of them the enemy. Had I been stopped and had they found the dynamite, I would have again faced a firing squad, without any doubt. I spoke to the person who answered the door. We only spoke the code words, "Orange above all," and I handed over my special goods. I turned around and travelled back to town. The dynamite was used to blow up the railroad just as a German military transport was travelling on the rails.

In the summer of 1942, I passed my final tests and received my high school diploma. Somehow, it had always been the plan that I would study medicine and I wanted to apply for the University of Amsterdam Medical School. The German government of the Netherlands had issued an order that one could only enter university in Holland after completing a six months course in special Nazi labor service. I did not want to do that and neither did all my friends. So I could not enter university. We got word however that in Amsterdam some professors quietly and unofficially lectured students at certain addresses. My father agreed with that scenario, and brought me and my buddy, Alfons Walder, to Amsterdam and found a rental room for both of us ("Fons" was an excellent student and later after WWII became professor of Neurosurgery at the University of Nijmegen and also was chosen to be the President of the International College of Neurosurgery). After settling down in our rental rooms, Fons and I were able to contact the people who ran the "underground" education for the University. We followed the clandestine lectures.

After a few months, however we moved to another

location mainly because of my "underground" activity. Two beautiful Jewish girls moved into another room and we were excited. I tried to romance one of them and remember reciting a poem to her by the French poet Ronsard. The poem was called à Hélene. Hélene in her old age reminisces about Ronsard offering his love to her when they were both younger and how she regrets not having appreciated and responding to his love. I had learned this poem by heart when I was in high school in Breda and had recited it at a literary competition. My almost "girlfriend" politely listened to my presentation but was not otherwise impressed. Well... I tried.

While in Amsterdam I became more and more involved in "underground" activities and must confess that I did not take the secret lectures very seriously (in contrast to Fons who ended up being one and a half years ahead of me in medical school). Again direct violent sabotage against the Germans was difficult for us in the underground. I was active in secretly bringing food and/or food stamps to mostly Jewish people hiding in secret homes. People whom the Germans tried to round up and send to concentration camps in Germany.

At first, the Jews had to wear a large yellow cross on their clothing if they went out and walked the streets, identifying them as Jews. Later they were all arrested and shipped by train in large numbers eastward to the German concentration camps. Amsterdam had a Jewish population of about 250,000.

One day I remember looking out the window on the fourth floor of my rental room down onto the street and saw the German Green Police patrolling the street and going into several homes looking for Jews. Some may have read the famous stories of Corrie ten Boom's. Corrie lived in Haarlem (yes after which Harlem, New York is named) with her father and sister. She hid several Jewish people (she was not Jewish herself) in the upper floors of her home.

She was betrayed and everybody arrested. They all ended up in a German concentration camp, where everyone died except Corrie. I never met Corrie, but we did similar work only about 12 miles from each other.

So, my job was to try to make sure that the hidden Jews had food. Therefore it was my task to go around Amsterdam and deliver food and or foodstamps to these people. Ann Frank's home was one of my destinations (after the war, her book, The Diary of Ann Frank and the movie of that book became world famous). I never met Ann because all of our work was top secret. We said as little as possible to anyone.

Around this time, I felt somewhat uneasy about my illegal work because of certain rumors. I decided to move back home, to Breda. It was too risky to move back in with my parents. It was as if God had warned me. Later on, I learned that the day after I moved from Amsterdam, German police officers came to the house looking for me. I had once again escaped a firing squad. This was the third time that I came close to the death penalty. It appeared that the Lord had other plans for me.

I moved back south to Breda. I stayed home with my parents sometimes. If I had known about my close arrest in Amsterdam I probably would never had stayed in their home (we did not have that knowledge and in retrospect, access to information in that time was not what it is now, where any bureaucrat can touch a few buttons on the internet and have a list of all your bank accounts, investments and the size of your underwear).

I was back home. The time was early 1944. I felt ashamed. I did not earn even a penny at the time. My life did not cost very much and my dear dad faithfully paid my way. Did he admire me because of my work in the underground? He never said so and we'll never know for sure.

I know I am not the only person who feels much love and gratitude for my parents many years later and I feel ashamed that I never expressed it at the time. I look forward to meeting them in heaven and express to them my deep appreciation for what they did at a time when I took them for granted.

We followed the world news on our little hidden radios very closely. The allies landed in Sicily and crossed the water onto the Italian mainland. The force consisted of Americans, British, Australian and Polish troops. They made a slow march north toward Naples and Rome.

In the Pacific, American marines fought hard and died hard, but they made progress from island to island. From what I understand, both John Kennedy and George Bush Senior served in the military operations in the Pacific.

The Soviet Army pushed the Germans back westward. Most of us did not know about communism until later or we did not think that it was very important, so we cheered the Russians on as they made progress. In Spain, General Franco was Hitler's friend but militarily he was not very active outside Spain's borders. Gibraltar I believe remained in British hands all through WWII, which was a blessing because that allowed allied traffic to enter and exit the Mediterranean Sea.

The British once did a very clever thing. They dumped the dead body of a British officer (who died in the war) just off the coast of Southern Spain. This body washed ashore and Spain turned the body over to the German Army. The Germans discovered a number of documents on the deceased Brit, strongly indicating British plans to start a landing operation and invasion in the near future somewhere at a certain spot on the French coast. This induced the Germans to concentrate a major part of their forces in that area. D-day was successful in part because the landing was at a totally different spot than the Germans had prepared for.

As we followed the progress of the allied forces throughout the world, we were excited to see a light at the end of the tunnel. The big day finally came. D-day June 6, 1944. Eisenhower landed thousands of allied troops on the coast of Normandy. You can imagine how elated we were and how we celebrated. Normandy was about three hundred miles from Breda. Many nations, other than American and British, participated in the Normandy operation and had all been organized and trained in Britain. The Dutch contributed the Irene Brigade, named after the Dutch princess Irene (Queen Juliana and Prince Bernhard's daughter). Our Underground forces, which still operated in occupied territory, were officially recognized as a military force and our commander was Prince Bernhard (even though he was still in Britain). This gave us a morale boost and pride. We felt that freedom would come fairly soon.

During July, August and September of 1944 the allied troops moved Eastward toward the Rhine River (under the great General Patton) and Northward into Northern France, Belgium and then finally the Netherlands. We followed all these movements with baited breath listening to the BBC from London. September 17 1944 became an historic day. The allied troops were somewhere south of us hung up in Belgium. Eisenhower and Montgomery (the top British General) planned a special operation, called "Operation Market Garden", whereby they would land troops just north of Breda in the province of Brabant and also further East towards Nijmegen and Arnhem. The land forces would push northward and join with the paratroopers forces to conquer a big wedge of Southern Holland, hoping to up the end of the war.

We saw the gliders go over us pulled by another plane and let loose in order to land and discharge troops and vehicles. The operation was partly successful but the main object (the occupation of Arnhem) was not achieved. In order to conquer Arnhem the troops had to cross the huge Rhine River. We were later told that treason was involved and that the Germans were notified of the attack. The

Germans were able to stop the allies from crossing the Rhine River. The Eastern part of Brabant (our province) was liberated September and the Southern part of the Limburg province to the East, where the city of Maastricht is, was not liberated until September 15 1944.

We, in the Western half of Brabant were still occupied. Needless to say our activities in the underground increased during those days. We passed a lot of information to the Allies, which helped them with their planning.

I must speak here of a very tragic happening. My very close buddy, Henk Hofman, who was the student president in high school, was, like me, a member of the Underground Army. We were in separate units. He was stationed in a small house, in the middle of the forest, close to our city. He was in the company of about a dozen others and they had a very good operation going. They would radio important information to the Allied troops, which were then only some twenty to thirty miles away. Someone found out about them and turned them in. The German Army surrounded the house and a gun battle followed. Our friends capitulated and were taken away.

The next day they were all executed by firing squad, two weeks before the liberation of our city. While they stood there, they all bravely shouted "long live the Queen". I visited Henk's body the next day at his parents' home. A bullet hole marred his forehead. I have been in North America since 1954 and have only been back in Europe three times. Each

35

time I visit Henk's grave and pray for his soul. He was a very, very fine man.

My View of History

In all Western occupied countries, such as Belgium, France, Denmark and Norway young people had formed underground forces against the German occupiers. In France, they were called the Maquis. The Maquis members were mostly communists.

From 1940-1945 all through WWII, the Soviets were on our side, fighting against Hitler coming from the East. The United States supplied Moscow overwhelmingly with weapons, tanks etc. which were shipped at great cost in convoys from the U.S. along the Northern Atlantic, northwards around Greenland, Iceland and Norway and delivered to the Soviet City of Murmansk. This may actually have been the greatest factor in the Russians beating the Germans in WWII.

The Germans occupied the Netherlands within five to seven days because of their overwhelming military superiority.

Some Dutch military personnel managed to escape across the North Sea to Britain. Our royal family, Queen Wilhelmina, her daughter princess Juliana and her husband prince Bernhard (who was of German origin) and their daughter princess Beatrix, who was born in 1939 (and is now Queen of the Netherlands as we write this) all managed to get away to Britain before the German Army could capture them. Queen Wilhelmina stayed in Britain during the war but princes Juliana and her family moved to Canada where they stayed during the remainder of the war. Princes Juliana's second daughter was born in Canada. The girl had a permanent partial eyesight loss because her mother had rubella (German measles) during her pregnancy.

Britain became a staging area during World War II where soldiers and airmen from other countries were organized. Some of the Dutch Military personnel gathered there. Canada sent over several divisions, the French had large contingents, who were under the command of General de Gaulle who later became the President of France.

Somehow, thousands of Polish military personnel managed to find their way to Britain. They had escaped the German-Soviet occupation of 1939 and found their way west via the Middle East. This is how there came to be more than one Polish Division in England. They fought in North Africa under the Polish General Anders, who later brought his division across the Mediterranean and joined with British and American forces to liberate Italy. A large contingent of Polish pilots came to England and played a heroic role in the Royal Air Force. The first Polish Tank Division in combination with a Canadian Division liberated our home town of Breda in October 1944.

During the German occupation our Dutch Government still functioned, but under strict German orders. We had a Dutch National Socialist Party, or NSB. The NSB consisted of a relatively small number of Dutch people who sympathized with Adolf Hitler. These people were now in charge of the country under German guidance and were hated by the general population. Their supreme leader was Mr. Mussert. The leader of the "Nazi" party in Norway was Mr. Quisling, whose name as a general traitor was and is still well known in Western literature. I believe Mr. Mussert was executed in Holland after WWII, an extremely exceptional case of the death penalty in Holland.

After World War II Corrie Ten Boom eventually moved to the U.S. where she gained fame with her book. She lived her last few years in California.

It is almost a scary thought that after December of 1941 and Pearl Harbor, the battle at Midway Island not far from Hawaii, which took place about May of 1942, was a tremendous victory for the U.S. when 4 Japanese aircraft carriers were sunk. This victory turned things around and was almost decisive for the eventual outcome of WWII. Three cheers for Admiral Nimitz. Then to think that the victory was partly based on luck and the right secret information about the enemy at the right time.

Henk Hofman, my close buddy, member of the Dutch under-ground, executed by a German firing squad on Oct 14' 44 two weeks before the liberation of Breda by Polish and Canadian troops (part of British Army).

Typical scenery of German cities (heavily bombed by the Allied Air Forces), which I viewed as we drove through them with the British Army in late 44' and early 45'.

During the German occupation an illegal (underground) newspaper circulated in Holland. Here under the heading: "Faithful" it lists the names of several Breda's citizens (hostages) executed by the German Army to set an example of "who is in charge and don't you dare do any harm to your occupiers". This was done at random to frighten the citizens. Above it says: "Faithful unto death".

*1945 Germany with my friends in the
British Army (I am in front center).*

*While I was recovering from surgery I embroidered
this in the British hospital in Germany.*

Christmas card sent to all British troops at Christmas 44' in Germany (far left the Canadian Army, next the Yorkshire Division, next "Movement Control"), next the Highland (Scottish Division), next the Polish Division. I am not sure about the last two.

On leave in Breda. Purely by coincidence my brother Robbert is also on leave from the U.S., where he was trained as a marine at Camp Le Jeune. Our little sister (Anne Marie) is betweern us. Early 1945

1945 as a member of the British Arm in Germany.

I am "fraternizing" with two German children.

Early 1945 as a patient in the British General Hospital in Germany. Purley by coincidence my older sister Elizabeth was admitted to the same hospital with the same illness from a totally different part of Germany, where she was also a member of the British Army.

CHAPTER III
The Liberation of Our Country

A few days before our liberation, I was on an assignment with my brother Robert to check out German gun positions in order to pass on the information to the other side. We found ourselves under grenade fire from the liberating forces as we hid in a dry ditch. I got hit in the left side of my neck with a piece of shrapnel. My brother stopped the bleeding with his thumb.

Shortly thereafter the firing died down and we went to a house nearby for help. The Red Cross came and transported me by bicycle to the nearest hospital. There was no modern ambulance. The Red Cross bicycle pulled a small wagon with a mattress upon which I lay. The hospital was close to our home.

The staff there cleaned and dressed my wound taking an X-ray, which showed a piece of shrapnel close to my spine. Since the city was in the middle of a warzone, the hospital staff was at a minimum and they decided not to do surgery to remove the shrapnel. After my discharge, my father and brother picked me up taking me to our home two blocks away. At home, we were in a warlike mode. The allied troops were close and we huddled as a family in the basement of our home. It was October 30 1944. Three days earlier we had seen large German columns, somewhat disheveled looking, moving in large numbers on their way East back to Germany. Small tanks, cars, bicycles and foot soldiers passed on the other side of the small lake in front of our house.

However, on this day grenades flew high overhead. From our basement, we looked outside onto the street through a small high window. A couple of soldiers in unusual uniforms jumped into our front yard with their rifles drawn. We heard them speak a language which none of us recognized. We later learned that they were soldiers of the First Polish Tank Division, which was part of General Montgomery's British Army. We were extremely excited: We were being liberated!

A few hours later, when things simmered down somewhat, we invited some of the Polish troops inside. We embraced them and my mother gave them coffee or tea and something to eat. We conversed with them the best we (and they) could in English or German.

Hurray! We were now a free country again. The Polish Army occupied our city for a while with the Canadian Army. Many local girls ended up marring the liberating soldiers.

The Polish Army set up a small field hospital not far from our home. I went there with my neck injury and was checked by a Polish surgeon. X-rays revealed a piece of shrapnel located one inch from my spinal cord. Once again, God had determined that my time had not come. If the shrapnel had moved one inch further it would have cut my spinal cord ending, almost certainly, in my demise.

The Polish military personnel were very nice to me; especially once they found out, I was a member of the Dutch Underground. I was treated with respect as a fellow soldier. I still have some uniform patches from the Polish soldiers as a souvenir. All Dutch Underground Army soldiers were eventually recognized as part of the Allied forces. We were officially under command of Prince Bernhard. We were issued special documents to carry in our wallets and special red-white-blue armbands to wear wherever we went. Although we did not have official uniforms, we were also issued rifles.

One of my assignments was to go to a nearby forest and work side by side with the Allied soldiers, carrying my rifle. We had to check the forest for hiding German soldiers.

The South of Holland had now been liberated. The Rhine River, coming from Western Germany, curves entering the Netherlands on the Eastern border, from East to West ending at Rotterdam, which is one of the largest harbors in the world. All ships wanting to travel the Oceans enter the North Sea from Rotterdam and then the Atlantic Ocean. The Rhine River flows from East to West cutting the Netherlands in two parts, with two-thirds of the country lying north of the Rhine and one-third south of the Rhine. At the end of October 1944, the Allies had liberated the Southern third of Holland, along with my hometown.

The Northern two-thirds of the country had to wait until May 1945. Many of our loved ones and friends lived in that part of the country.

My older sister, who was a nurse, was one of them. She worked in a hospital in the city of Utrecht. Later on when we were unified she told us horror stories of hunger and deprivation. Northern Holland went through one of the worst periods of its history from October 1944 to May 1945. I heard stories of people eating rats, tulip bulbs and weeds or grass.

After October 1944 in Breda, I did some military assignments as a member of the underground army but the war was still going on. The Allies had barely begun to enter Germany itself and the German Army was still a major force to be reckoned with.

In December 1944, a major battle took place 200 miles southeast of my hometown. It would later be called the Battle of the Bulge. It took place in Eastern Belgium. It happened to be one of the most severe winters in history. It was very cold and snow covered the ground. Thousands of soldiers on both sides lost their lives.

While this was going on I was in hospital with appendicitis and had to have an appendectomy. We tried anxiously to follow the news on T.V. and in the newspapers, which were now free to report the news honestly, no longer with a Nazi slant.

CHAPTER IV
Joining the British Army

After recovering from surgery at home, I got word that the British Army was looking for interpreters. In high school, I had learned German, English and French (Apparently in Britain, the teaching of the continental languages was not a great priority and most British officers only spoke English). I eagerly applied for this assignment.

At the command post, with about ten other young men, I got basic military training. I remember the British Sergeant reprimanding one of the trainees for having no crease in his pants. The young man protested that his pants were "full of creases". Needless to say, he was pretty well roughed up after that remark.

Our training period lasted a few weeks. We interpreters were then split up and taken to different military units. I was shipped south to Brussels and then taken to British Movement Control (run by the British Engineers). We were involved with railroad transportation and we followed closely behind the front line of the war along railroad tracks and railway stations. From Brussels, I went with a small convoy of British Royal Engineers, going through Northern Belgium passing through Southern Holland toward the northeast into Western Germany.

We travelled further North and participated in the liberation of a Dutch City (I believe Enschede) in Eastern Holland close to the German border. We made our way through the main streets of the city in a column of marching soldiers and riding vehicles. A crowd of thousands of waving and cheering people, who were exhilarated to have survived the war, overwhelmed us. They treated us like heroes and we felt like heroes. I strongly believe that next to our faith in God, freedom is the most precious thing in life, and the hardest to keep.

Officially, I was a member of the Dutch Army Corps of Interpreters, but I was attached to the British Army as a sergeant interpreter and paid by the British Army. From Enschede in about January 1945, we moved further east and somewhat north into Germany. We passed through towns and cities and the sight shocked me. All these towns were practically destroyed by the Allied bombing, which had taken place over the last two years. It was a sight, which I will never forget.

We saw disheveled people shoveling along the streets looking through the rubble. We saw this sight repeatedly everywhere we travelled. Germany was our enemy but I couldn't help feeling sorry for the people. The carpet-bombings not only caused enormous destruction but also killed hundreds of thousands, including women and children.

I clearly remember a few months earlier seeing literally hundreds of bombers, escorted by fighters coming from England, darkening the sky over our hometown, on their way to Germany to do their job. This was a major factor in bringing the Nazis to their knees.

At the time, I was of course anti-German. I can't help feeling that nowadays there would have been moral outrage.

The front line of the war crawled eastward, with the Germans retreating, us following close behind. We stayed in different camps or small towns overnight and packed up the next morning, moving on. Because of the nature of our unit, we stayed close to railway tracks and railway stations. We saw trains packed with thousands of Western people (French, Belgians, and Dutch). The German Army had taken these people to work in German factories because of a huge shortage of manpower. Now they were liberated heading back home to the West. One can only imagine how happy these people were. When they stopped at our station, they were fed and I had many interesting conversations with them.

During the war the Germans who were fighting in the East, in Russia, also took many thousands of Eastern civilians back into Germany to work. These people were to be shipped back East to Poland and the Soviet Union. After the war ended, the Eastern people were far less enthusiastic to go home because it meant returning to communism. A large train, packed mostly with Russians, stopped at our station. We fed them and took care of their needs. Some of them wandered farther from the train. They raped some women, stole small cattle and plundered the storage sheds that housed supplies used to feed people from passing trains. I called all the people onto the platform and gave a short speech in German with a few Russian words (my Russian was very limited). I told them that we English people were their friends and this behavior would not be tolerated. After that the situation improved somewhat.

We moved further eastwards and I stayed in Goslar for a while, a small town in the Harz Mountains. What a fairy tale like scenery.

From here, we moved north and were stationed at Rotenfelde-Wolfsburg. This small town was located at a canal. On the other side of the canal sat the huge Volkswagen factory. What an eerie sight--huge factory buildings stretched for perhaps half a mile, totally abandoned, totally silent.

On our side of the canal was a large camp, in which many refugees lived, men and women, all taken by the Germans from the Eastern countries into Germany to work. Now they were all free and were supposed to go home. We were invited to parties in their camp. The joy was so great, I loved the wonderful music (Russian and Polish) and the vodka was nice. I learned from the Russians to drink a glass, empty it in one swallow (VSHO!), and throw the glass in the fire. They loved drinking and celebrating but I had to use my self-control in order not to get carried away and get sick.

I met a beautiful Polish lady of my age, fell in love and after a few months married her in a small German town. She wore a uniform because she had been a member of the Polish Underground in Warsaw. The Germans and the Russians of course had invaded Poland in 1939.

In early May 1945, Germany surrendered. The war was officially over. My unit moved again and we were stationed at the town of Helmstedt.

West Germany was divided into 4 zones. Going from north to south you had the French zone, the Canadian zone, the British zone and the American zone. Helmstedt, in the British zone, was located right at the demarcation line. On the other side of the line was the Soviet Army. Our British officers had to negotiate from time to time with the Soviet command over border issues and I had to translate. The top Russian officers spoke either German or French so we used one of these languages due to my limited Russian.

I enjoyed a pleasant life with the British Army. Most soldiers and officers treated me well. I had problems understanding the regional accents of the men. There spoke cockney from the London area and Scottish and Welsh and then all the many accents in between. At meal times, the language could be quite a nightmare, but I gradually got used to it.

One can imagine the rage I still felt against the German Army. They had brutalized my country and killed my best friend. The British officers were very "correct" and treated the Germans and German prisoners rather "properly."

Once, my English friends in our unit talked me into going with them to a German town. They wanted to search homes and confiscate radios. They needed me to translate. I was reluctant to do it but finally broke down. We went to the town with a truck, entered several homes and took some loot. When we returned to the barracks, one of the British officers got wind of what we had done and ordered us to go back and return all the confiscated items. It was a good lesson in humility.

An officer overheard me yelling and berating a German prisoner. I was punished with two days of CB (Confined to Barracks) and had to polish several pairs of boots.

One day I was patrolling a country road, accompanied by a few British soldiers. We were near the American zone adjacent to the British zone when we encountered a small group of American military personnel. They fired their guns trying to hit a can on the top of a pole quite a distance away. I carried my stengun, which some may know is like a small machinegun. It is not designed for sharp shooting, more for spraying a bunch of bullets at the enemy.

I asked, "May I take a shot?"

They laughed when they saw my stengun. "Okay, go ahead."

I took aim and fired one bullet through the can. The Americans were impressed. I wished them well and went on my way.

I believe that every person has feel-good moments in life. They are rare but sure feel good.

I got a few days leave and went home to Breda by train. I couldn't wait to see my parents and tell them all about my military life. When I went home, I was surprised that my brother Robert had come home on leave at the same time, purely by coincidence. He had been assigned as a marine and was sent to Camp Lejeune in the U.S. for training. What a joyous reunion! I took pride in the fact that as a sergeant I outranked my brother.

I returned to Helmstedt. We were positioned on the railroad track. A few yards to the east was the Russian Army. Trains came from the east rolling into our zone, after the Soviets had inspected them. Many trains had open wagons filled with potatoes or coal. In many cases, once the train cars were safely on the Western side, people crawled out from under the coal or potatoes, excited that they were able to escape from communism. (Ironically, now, about 70 years later, people vote for communism in the U.S. without realizing it).

Some of the trains carried hundreds of people who came out of German concentration camps. They stood in open wagons, very thin and pale. What an unforgettable sight. These people were not all Jews, but were returning home to France, Belgium or Holland. I talked to many of these people as well as to others who managed to make it to the west over land. After the notorious wall went up on the East German side the foot traffic of fleeing people came to a brutal halt.

Hundreds of people told me about the horrible things they had gone through when the Russian Army "liberated" a Polish or East German town. They erased everything they could see. Women were raped and many drowned themselves in nearby lakes or rivers to avoid further abuse. Their homes were ransacked and everything of value stolen. People were killed at random and the cattle were slaughtered.

The worst story I heard came from Berlin. The Russian Army liberated Berlin. They came upon a special school for teenage girls and young women. What happened there has been recorded and I have the story tucked away at home. The things that were done there were so heinous and horrible, that I cannot bring myself to write them down. Suffice it to say, almost none of the women survived.

Twice while in the British Army, I was hospitalized. The British General Military hospital was located some 100 miles from where we were stationed. The shrapnel in my neck had been bothering me, so I was sent to that hospital, where they surgically removed the grenade piece from my neck.

The surgeons commented how extremely lucky I was that the piece had not gone one inch further, which would have meant my demise. They gave me the shrapnel in a glass tube, which I later gave to my mother (unfortunately it got lost when my parents moved to another house).

My second hospital admission was quite different. I contracted "rubella" (German measles) which did not get much better in a few days so I was taken again to the same hospital.

While I was lying in my hospital bed the British doctor in charge made his rounds and when he spoke to me he said, "There is another patient, a young woman on the next floor up who not only has the same illness as you, but she has the same last name."

I was flabbergasted. I went to visit the mystery patient on the next floor. It was my sister! We screamed and embraced. She was the nurse mentioned earlier, who had been liberated in May 1945 while working in the hospital in Utrecht.

She told me she had volunteered for the British Army. She was very good with her languages and got assigned to a Censorship Unit located somewhere in West Germany. She read letters written by German prisoners to their friends and loved ones in order to find anything suspect before forwarding the letters to their destination. My sister, Elizabeth (or Liesje as we called her), and I had a lot to talk about. The coincidence of us being in the same place with the same diagnosis was a totally unexpected delight.

Liesje also fell in love during the war. She met a nice and sharp young Czech gentleman, Freddy, who did the same job as she in the Censorship Unit. Freddie had escaped Czecho-Slovakia in the late thirties, during Hitler's invasion of his country. He made his way to England and joined the British Army.

Liesje and Freddie were married and settled in England. A couple of years later they immigrated to Australia where they stayed the rest of their lives. They had two children and ran a successful business in antiques. I visited them a couple of times over the years. Freddie died a few years ago and Liesje died just a few weeks before the time of this writing (June 2012).

Although she never went to university to obtain a masters degree, she was sharp and self taught. She specialized in classical languages, Latin and Greek

57

and obtained a bachelor's degree from an Australian University. The few times I saw her after World War II, I very much enjoyed our conversations about life, religion, philosophy, and psychology.

I visited Polish/Ukrainian refugee camps. These were not the same as concentration camps, with strict and brutal discipline, and poor, if any, food. The concentration camps were mostly populated by Jews, who had been arrested by the German forces from all over Europe.

While I was in high school, I had two Jewish teachers, one for the French language and one for Latin. They were both excellent teachers, and looking back, I have nothing but deep gratitude and admiration for their skill and devotion to teaching us. Both these gentlemen were taken to a German concentration camp and we never saw them again. (In their honor I will mention their names: Mr. Gokkes for French and Mr. Stein for Latin).

The other people in concentration camps were arrested, usually for activities in the underground (sabotage, helping Jews etc.). For my activities, I almost certainly would have been executed if I had been caught, but I also could have been taken to a concentration camp.

The refugee/worker camps in Germany mostly contained civilians from East and West European countries. Since most of the young German people were taken in by the military, there was a huge shortage of workers, needed in the German industry and factories, so the German military brought as many people from the occupied countries into

Germany to work. Krystyna, my wife, was one of those people. She was, as most Polish people are, a very brave young lady and participated in the Polish Underground for a short period while she was in Warsaw, prior to be taken into Germany.

My View of History

The strongest attempt in world history to recognize the importance and the essence of freedom, I believe, was laid down in the American Declaration of Independence and the Constitution. No other country in world history ever came that close and that is why this country is "special" and unique. Unfortunately, many Americans don't realize this and even laugh at our country being called special. Our freedom has slowly been diminished in the last few years by creeping socialism and suffocating regulation. One would think that communist countries are the least "free" nations and essentially that is true. However, we are moving toward a more and more oppressive society, which could be worse than communism.

Let me give you an example. My present wife, was born and lived in most of her life in communist mainland China, went a year ago to visit her mother in Hohhot in the province of Inner Mongolia. She took my Chinese adopted son, his American wife and the two grandchildren with her. Sometimes they travelled in a car. The cars all had seatbelts. Here, in the U.S.A. if you get stopped and are not wearing a seatbelt you are fined. In China, the police do not care whether you wear your belt or not. My four year old grandson Joshua in America must sit in a government designed regulated car seat in the back. In China, he sat on grandma's lap in the back seat shouting, "I am free, I am free." So we are more regulated than China.

Regarding the people who did not want to return home after the war, I had made friends with some Soviet officers and we exchanged addresses. After the war, long after I was back home I tried to write to my Russian friends. I never got any answers. I learned it was the policy of the Soviets to have most of their military personnel who had seen the much more free West "disappear" once they came back home to Russia. They had tasted the Western way of life and had been "polluted" by western freedom.

Particularly the Polish did not want to go "home" because they knew that the Red Army occupied Poland. Perhaps a million Polish people ended up finally in England, Canada, the U.S. and Australia. One can only imagine how horrible the thought of living under communism must have been not to return to your own home.

As most people know, Germany was divided in two halves by a demarcation line running from North to South through Germany. This divided Germany into West and East Germany. East Germany was occupied by the Soviets and became a communist country. The Soviets built a wall along the demarcation line with the main purpose of stopping people from fleeing from East to West. In the over 40 years of the existence of this wall over five thousand people managed to go over, under, or through it.

Today we are told that we cannot build a wall at our Southern border to stop the flood of illegal Mexican's.

I want to emphasize that the droves of people from the East that tried to make it to West (freedom), millions never made it and were stuck in communist Poland and East Germany for the next 40 years.

It should be noted that the American General Patton was almost alone in foreseeing that Soviet Communism would conquer Eastern Europe and force communism on those countries for years to come. Patton made it very clear that now was the time to push further east and defeat the Soviet Army. The Soviets had millions of soldiers but the Allies were extremely better equipped in armaments. Not following Patton's advice tragically meant that all Eastern European countries would be condemned to about 4 decades of communist dictatorship.

As I said before, the devastation of West German cities by the Allied bombing was practically total. However, the Germans are such amazing hard workers, and with the allies' participation in The Marshall Plan to restore Europe, the clean up and rebuilding was done faster that anyone's expectation.

Amsterdam 1946 - 54' studying medicine. I lived in a small apartment on the 5th floor very close to this picture.

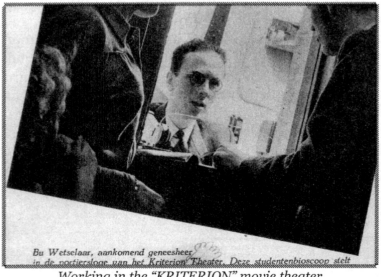

Bu Wetselaar, aankomend geneesheer
in de portierslage van het Kriterion Theater. Deze studentenbioscoop stelt

*Working in the "KRITERION" movie theater
to support my family while studying.*

*Working as an intern/resident in St. Joseph's
Hospital, Victoria, B.C., Canada 1954-56.*

*On our day off, Vancouver, B.C. with my colleague and special
friend Jack Sevensma, who became an anesthesiologist.*

I travelled on the hospital ship Columbia, calling on small mountain settlements and Indian Villages. There is the pastor who travelled with us and went ashore to talk with families. 1955.

Typical shore scene from the Columbia.

1955

With the pastor on our ship.

Canada 1956-57 making house calls.
The ferry took my car across the Fraser River.

The Fraser River - when I practiced in
Lytton, B.C. my first practice 1956 - 57'.

The favorite way to transport a patient from
British Columbia's coastal inlets to a Vancouver hospital.

Our hospital ship traveling to the next Indian Village.

View from our hospital ship 1955 - 56.

One of British Columbia's main industries: logging; transporting big floats from up North to Vancouver 1955.

Practicing in the Canadian Artic. Ready to mount the dog sleigh to make a house call.

WIND CHILL CHART
CURRENT TEMPERTURE

0	35	30	25	20	15	10	5	0	-5	-10	-15	-20	-25	-30	-35	-40	-45
5	33	27	21	16	12	7	1	-6	-11	-15	-20	-26	-31	-35	-41	-47	-54
10	21	16	9	2	-2	-9	-15	-22	-27	-31	-38	-45	-52	-58	-64	-70	-77
15	16	11	1	-6	-11	-18	-25	-33	-40	-45	-51	-60	-65	-70	-78	-85	-90
20	12	3	-4	-9	-17	-24	-32	-40	-46	-52	-60	-68	-76	-81	-88	-96	-103
25	7	0	-7	-15	-22	-29	-37	-45	-52	-58	-67	-75	-83	-89	-96	-104	-112
30	5	-2	-11	-18	-26	-33	-41	-49	-56	-63	-70	-78	-87	-94	-101	-109	-117
35	3	-4	-13	-20	-27	-35	-43	-52	-60	-67	-72	-83	-90	-98	-105	-113	-123
40	1	-4	-15	-22	-29	-36	-45	-54	-62	-69	-76	-87	-94	-101	-107	-116	-128
45	1	-6	-17	-24	-31	-38	-46	-54	-63	-70	-78	-87	-94	-101	-108	-118	-128
50	0	-7	-17	-24	-31	-38	-47	-56	-63	-70	-79	-88	-96	-103	-110	-120	-128

(Left axis: WIND IN MILES PER HOUR)

Find the current temperature on the top line. Move down the line to point opposite the present wind velocity. This is the equivalent temperature under such wind conditions.

Wind chill chart for the Arctic. N.W.T stands for the Canadian province of "North West Territories" bordering on the Arctic Ocean and on Alaska.

1984 Visiting Indonesia to visit my brother and on my way to Australia to visit my sister. Traveling on Java I ran into a bunch of children, who just got out of school.

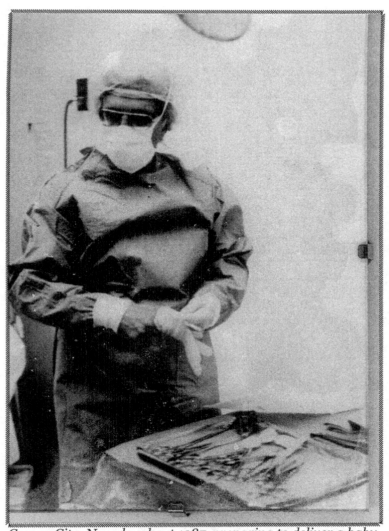

Carson City, Nevada, about 1987, preparing to deliver a baby.

CHAPTER V
End of the War
Going Back Home

I had planned to stay with the British Army as an interpreter after the war, hoping to be promoted and improve my language skills. I especially wanted to learn more Polish and Russian. Imagine my shock when early in 1946, my officers told me that I had done a good job but now the war was over and they didn't need me anymore.

I boarded a train with my new wife and headed to Holland. Back home I introduced my wife to my parents. Then my new reality sank in.

What am I going to do?

I could tell that my parents, especially my mother, were not very happy and she let me know. To study at a University, being married and expecting our first child, was a ridiculous thought at that time in Holland.

A relative gave me a job at an advertising agency in Amsterdam, so that is where my wife and I settled.

The attitude of my parents was clear. When one studied at a university, it is custom in Holland for your father to be responsible financially. However, once you got married, you are on your own. It was thought impossible to raise a family and study at the university at the same time.

I started my new job in Amsterdam and we found a small apartment on the fourth floor, in an old building with no elevator, on one of Amsterdam's famous canals.

I spent some time in my new job when I received some exciting information. There was a movie theater in town, owned by student-leaders. All of the employees were students at the University of Amsterdam. The shifts were usually mid to late afternoon and weekends, so the students were able to attend daytime lectures at the University.

I got on my bike, applied at the theater (called "KRITERION") and was accepted! We were thrilled. I subsequently attended the University of Amsterdam Medical School. In my youthful optimism, I never realized the enormity of this new undertaking. Later on, my parents and other relatives told me that nobody expected me to succeed at studying medicine and raising a family.

I enjoyed my job at "KRITERION" selling tickets and being an usher. I met my colleagues who were also students, several in subjects other than medicine. We had very interesting discussions about politics, religion, psychology and many other topics. My salary was very little, but we scraped by. My grandfather, who was secretly impressed with my efforts, sent me 75 guilders a month to help us.

I joined the Amsterdam Student Corps, which

was a student social organization. Like the University itself, this was a very old (about 100 years) society and it was an honor to belong to it. To join this society we had to go through hazing. We were shown a plate of worms, then blindfolded and told to eat the worms. The plate of worms was quietly changed to a plate of spaghetti while we were blindfolded. After the hazing, we were usually accepted as new members of the society. Once accepted, you are a member for life (I still get newsletters) and it is considered quite an honor.

At the university, we had different groups of students--Catholic, Protestant, Socialist and Communist. We debated furiously. I found myself initially drawn to socialism, because it seemed fair that those who were not too well off should be helped by those who were. Later on, over the next few years I moved gradually toward the right and became a conservative.

We lived in our tiny apartment, two rooms and a "kitchen" (which was full with two people in it) on the fourth floor, with our bicycles downstairs in a shed. One floor higher up was a small attic, where I studied, often with a friend, so we could rehearse and test each other.

My main pal was Jack Sevensma, a wonderful, good-hearted young man. Like me, Jack later on immigrated to Canada, got married and worked as a physician/anesthesiologist in Ontario (he died of leukemia about 20 years ago. I miss him very much).

My son, Henri Jr., was born in 1946 and brought us great love and pleasure. It was good exercise to carry a baby up and down four floors. I remember studying in the little, low-ceilinged attic. It was stifling hot without air conditioning. We put our feet in large pans of cold water and placed cold wraps on our foreheads. About one year later, I passed my first exam and my second one about two years later. My parents and other relatives were somewhat impressed.

We had a second child in 1950, a girl, Janina. Financially we were under greater strain but on the other hand, it increased our general family happiness.

In 1952 I passed the 'big one', my doctoral examination. Now, on paper, I was a doctor. I faced another two years of internship and residencies.

We were motivated to move to the U.S, Canada or Australia because Holland has socialized medicine like most of Europe. There appeared to be too many doctors in Holland. Through a friend, I heard of an opening for an internship in Victoria, British Columbia, Canada. I applied for an intern position at St. Joseph's Hospital in Victoria and was accepted.

In North America, I learned about the U.S.A. being so exceptional. Because it was based on the Declaration of Independence and the Bill of Rights. People had inalienable rights of freedom and freedom of speech and those rights were given by the Creator! What a unique exciting concept. All I had known so far were rights issued by kings or governments.

History from My View

It is interesting to note, the Abu Grebe scandal in Iraq in about 2002 that the (mostly liberal) press severely criticized the Bush administration for the scandalous, cruel treatment that was administered to the Iraqi prisoners by the terrible American military. The Iraqis were forced to wear women's clothes and had to crawl around, almost naked, like dogs. To me this whole matter was laughable because the above cruelties, and worse, were precisely what we went through in our hazing period.

CHAPTER VI
Starting a New Life in Canada

My wife and I decided that I would go alone to Canada to complete my internship. It would take me about a year to become a licensed physician and then my family would join me. My wonderful parents agreed to have my wife and two small children stay with them in Holland.

Before I left, my whole family went to visit the Canadian Embassy in The Hague. We were accepted as future immigrants after interviews and physical examinations. In midsummer of 1954, I boarded a large ocean liner for Canada. My family and my parents came to Rotterdam where I said goodbye to everyone.

During my journey across the Northern Atlantic, I met another young physician. It turned out that he was on his way to the same hospital in Victoria, British Columbia, to become an intern, too. Naturally, we had a lot to talk about.

After about 8 days, we arrived in Halifax, Nova Scotia and set foot on Canadian soil. Next, we had to travel to Montreal, the capital of Quebec. This was the only time I would ever set foot in Montreal. It is a beautiful, exciting city. The main language is French, which is the second official language of Canada so we practiced that for a short time.

A few days later, we boarded a Canadian Pacific Railway train. It took us all the way across the North American continent westward to Vancouver, British Columbia. This unforgettable trip took about 3 days across huge deserts, forests, mountains and prairies. The sight of thousands of miles of movie like nature left an awesome, deeply respectful feeling of admiration for God's creations in my mind and heart. I had travelled by train from Holland to Switzerland and Austria to go skiing with my father just before World War II and marveled at the mountains, but to experience the Canadian Rockies in Alberta and British Columbia blew me away.

After a nearly 3000-mile journey, we arrived in Vancouver, British Columbia, which lies on the Pacific Ocean. We had not yet arrived at our final destination. We were transported to Vancouver harbor where we boarded a ferry. This took us in a couple of hours to Vancouver Island, which is a huge cigar shaped island lying alongside the coast of British Columbia. We disembarked at Victoria, a wonderful, old city, which is the capital of the Province.

We were taken to our final destination--St, Joseph's Hospital (which I believe is now called Victoria General Hospital). We were welcomed to our one year internship, were given our schedules and shown to our rooms. Our year of duties would be split up in different specialty sections--Internal Medicine,

Surgery, Pediatrics and Obstetrics/Gynecology. We also had to take turns working in the Emergency room. Our meals where eaten in a doctor's dining room.

It was an exciting challenge to actually work as a doctor and to be looked up to by patients, who were in pain, feeling bad, emotionally upset or wounded. These people expected me to heal them. What a responsibility, what a challenge!

We had a small advantage over most other doctors. We frequently had to deal with European immigrants who spoke very little English. We could speak to them in Dutch, German or French.

Older local specialists-doctors, who taught us a lot, supervised us. I learned early on that good bedside manners and a good doctor-patient relationship are very important for a physician. One local doctor, let us call him Dr. G., was not particularly known for having the latest scientific knowledge readily available. He had one of the kindest, warmest personalities with his patients one could imagine.

Dr. G. had one of the largest practices in Victoria. When he came to visit his patients in our hospital, we always enjoyed working with him, more than the other doctors. As far as how to handle your patients on a personal basis he was, for us, the best teacher. We were very thankful that we also had top of the line scientific doctors to learn from. God bless them! They have advanced medical care in the world, especially in the last 50-100 years.

I learned so much in that year. Some occurrences stand out in my memory. Once, while I was on duty in the Emergency room a mother brought in a 3-year-old boy, who had swallowed a marble. The perfectly round item shot into his larynx instead of his esophagus, thus cutting of his lung passage. He could not breathe. We frantically tried to remove the marble but were not able to and the child died. He was unconscious when he arrived in our department. We were shocked and deeply saddened, and I will never forget that experience. The pain of the mother must have been indescribable. I now understand the loss she must have felt because I have a 5-year-old grandson. The love I feel for this little boy I can never describe in words. The thought that something so terrible could happen to him is scary and would be devastating. that I don't know if I would want to live myself after such an occurrence. The poor mother of that boy. I often wonder how she is doing now.

One of my duties was to do circumcisions on the newborn boys. I was taught how to do it and I believe that technically, I did a decent job, but emotionally I had a bit of a hard time. I had to cut and torture a tiny human being without anesthetic. I did it because I was told to but I always felt a little guilty and cruel. These babies are now men and I'd like to ask their forgiveness.

We had a doctors lounge where we relaxed for a while when we were off duty. I had wonderful conversations with the local Victoria doctors and learned so much from them. We often had the TV on and watched baseball or football, which was very popular. The local doctors taught me the rules. The World Series' and Super Bowls were watched with great excitement. My life changed so much in that first year.

When my year was over, I had to go to Winnipeg (Manitoba) to sit for a license exam. When I passed, I gained my L.M.C.C (Licentiate of the Medical Council of Canada). I could now practice medicine anywhere in Canada, after becoming a member of the Provincial Medical Board. I became a member of the "College of Physicians and Surgeons of British Columbia" in 1956 and am still a member to this day. A few years ago, the Province of B.C. passed a law, forbidding doctors over the age of 70 to practice medicine and see patients. One would argue that in the age of political correctness and severe condemnation of discrimination, this law is one of the most egregious examples of age-discrimination in the western world. Thank God, we don't have similar discrimination in the U.S. (I am still practicing at age 88).

In the summer of 1955, after my internship, I applied to stay on at the same hospital as a resident in Surgery and Obstetrics and Gynecology. I was accepted. Before starting my job, I took a few weeks' vacation.

My salary from the hospital in the first year was $150.00 per month so I didn't have much savings leftover. I managed to buy a 1936 Ford for $150.00. I was half owner; Dr. Love, who was an intern like me, owned the other half. We had a wonderful time with that car. The car had no heat, so in the winter, frost would form on the outside windshield, which made it practically impossible to drive. We solved that problem by lighting candles and putting them on the dashboard. This made the outside ice melt and gave us just enough vision to carry on carefully.

So I needed some money in the summer of 1955. Luckily, I heard about a possible job. The Anglican Church owned a small hospital ship, stationed in the Vancouver harbor. About twice a year, this ship would travel between Vancouver Island and the mainland, north. The trip took two to three weeks. On its journey, the ship brought medical care to the outlying coastal settlements and logging camps, which could mostly not be reached by land. Remote Indian villages were also serviced. It felt important; the people were so excited to have a medical doctor visit. Emergent medical problems had to be taken by seaplane to Vancouver.

The ship was about 100 feet long. The crew consisted of a captain, an engineer, a cook and a minister. The fifth person on board was the doctor. I applied for the job and was accepted. It would be the first time in my career I worked as a physician outside a hospital.

The water and scenery between Vancouver Island and the mainland were wonderful. We passed multiple islands, and off and on, we pulled into an inlet on the mainland coast. Those inlets were so huge that one could really call them fjords, like the ones into the Norwegian Coast. The inlet could be up to a mile wide and on both sides, the walls of the mountains rose up a few thousand feet. We heard the soft sound of our engine but otherwise there was an awesome silence. We felt like ants.

We came upon a conglomeration of several

floats, composed of logs tied together. On the floats were some primitive huts and small houses. These floating villages were tied onto the mainland in such a way that they would rise and fall with the ocean tides. The people living in these tiny communities were loggers. They cut down premium timbers on the mountainside, and slid them down the mountain into the ocean water. Then they tied the logs together into a huge float. Then, attached to a small motorboat, the whole assembly was dragged along the coast towards Vancouver where they sold the wood. Maneuvering this huge float took the work of a highly skilled log-skipper. The small floating village attached to the mountain was the workers' homes, where they lived with their families. They stayed at one spot a few months and then moved along the coast to another spot.

Upon our arrival at such a village, people were excited and some would come on board of our ship. The minister would hold religious services and pray with individuals. Then patients would come on board and nervously I started to practice medicine. The patients were usually very nice and appreciative. I was also the pharmacist, issuing prescriptions of medication from our supplies.

I found out that sometimes being doctor and pharmacist was not enough. I also had to be a dentist. There was an old dental book in my office with illustrations telling me precisely where to inject the anesthetic. There were also dental instruments and guidelines for choosing the right one to pull a particular tooth. I was nervous at first, but there was nobody else, so I went ahead and ended up pulling several teeth during my hospital trips.

Our ship stopped at a mountainside on which an Indian community was located. I treated the Indian adults and children. Some would come on board but we also visited some patients in their huts and primitive homes. Most Indians spoke some degree of English. I also learned some of their language (the British Columbia Coastal Indians). Toothache in their language is Gigi tsechiella. I used those words often.

When I was back in Victoria, I shared my stories with some older friends from Holland, who like my parents, many years ago had spent some time in Indonesia. When I told my older friend the above story she said, 'Well, let me tell you something interesting. The word for tooth in the Malayan (Indonesian) language is also Gigi.' How very interesting!

We travelled along British Columbia's coast. The boat sometimes slowed down or stopped if we had good weather. I would swim off the boat. Once we tied up at Alert Bay, a small settlement on an island just off the Northern tip of Vancouver Island. I hiked along the beach and found a huge vertebra, obviously from a whale. Later on, I gave this unusual item to my son. I took many photographs on this interesting journey and mailed them to one of my old friends in the Netherlands. He was very interested and planned to have them published in one of the Dutch newspapers. Unfortunately, the photo's got lost and my friend died soon thereafter.

After my ocean adventure, I returned to Victoria and started my one-year residency in Surgery and

Obstetrics in St. Joseph's Hospital. I learned a lot in a relatively short time, and delivered many babies.

I come now to a painful period to talk about but I feel I must be honest and open. In mid 1956, my family boarded an ocean liner in Holland, crossed the Atlantic and travelled by train, as I had two years earlier, all across Canada to Vancouver. I picked them up at the railway station in Vancouver with great excitement. We were united again. We crossed the water together on the ferry. I settled my family in a small apartment across from the hospital where I worked.

My wife and I apparently had grown so far apart in those two years that we had become incompatible. This was a disaster, especially for our two children. My family got settled in Victoria after schools were found for the children and I left town.

A family country practice was for sale in a small mountain town in Lytton, B.C. which was about one hundred and fifty miles North of Vancouver. It was located where two large rivers flowed together-- the Fraser River and the Thompson River. The local doctor, who was selling his practice, and I came to an agreement and I bought his practice for I believe $25,000.00. I never realized what a huge adventure I was getting into.

I bought a 1956 Meteor, made in the Canadian Ford factory back East, and rented a small house, which became my medical office as well. I briefly met the previous doctor and he left town. My practice consisted of about one thousand whites and one thousand Indians.

There was a small local hospital, complete with emergency room and operating/delivery room, called St. Bartholomew's Hospital. I believe the Anglican Church sponsored it. Since I was the only doctor, I immediately became medical director. I made rounds in the hospital, coverd the ER and saw patients in my own office.

I met wonderful interesting people. One was an old Dutchman who was a dowser. He would walk slowly over a certain piece of land holding a V like steel frame in front of him and find oil, gas or gold when the frame in his hands bent a certain way. I am not sure how true or scientific this was but people hired him.

I worked a lot with the local RCMP Station (Royal Canadian Mounted Police) and we became good friends. Sometimes I had to go to sites of accidents. Once a husband and wife drove their car on the freeway close to Lytton and, while going around a corner the husband got distracted by a bee in the car. He swerved, lost control and the car went over the bank towards the roaring Fraser River. Fortunately, the car slammed into a tree and got stuck. The RCMP called me to the site. I had to crawl down the bank to the car. We found the man alive but unfortunately, we had to pronounce the wife dead from the impact. We took the husband to the hospital, where I treated his wounds surgically and after a few days, he was released to a totally different life.

Once, in the middle of the night I was called to deliver an Indian baby. I got dressed and gathered my doctor's bag and tools, but in order to get to the woman involved I had to cross the Fraser River on a railway track, high above the water. I held the railing, which was only on one side and walked beside the track. If a train had passed I would have been only inches away from it, holding on to the railing, hoping the train would not hit me. There was no road or any other crossing for miles over the river other than that railroad track. I made it to the other side, found the small house, which was not easy in the forest, delivered the baby and managed to get home on the track.

I had found out what it was like to be a country doctor. I was supposed to be a family doctor but found out that I was supposed to be much more. The nearest other doctor was about a hundred miles away.

Once an Indian girl, about 6 or 7 years old, died from unknown causes. I received a strong request from the local coroner to do an autopsy. All of a sudden, I was a pathologist whether I liked it or not. I went ahead with the autopsy and concluded that the cause of death was pneumonia.

On another occasion, a young man was admitted to the hospital with appendicitis. He needed surgery, now. I had had my surgical training even though I was not a full surgeon. The second problem was that he had to be anesthetized for the surgery and I was not an anesthesiologist. I had no choice. I had to be both specialists. I turned the patient on his side, injected an anesthetic fluid into his spine, which froze the lower part of his body. After that, I turned him onto his back and I operated on him with the head-nurse as my assistant. God bless her. She was an English lady, highly skilled and a high-class person. The patient left the hospital a few days later feeling well.

Once a week I would drive south on the highway for about fifty miles and cross the river in a hanging cage which took my car to Boston Bar. In this small town, I made house calls, mostly to Indians. The Indians must have liked me, because after I left Lytton around 1958, the leaders of the local Indian tribe wrote a letter to the Minister of Health of British Columbia asking if there was any way to bring Dr. Wetselaar back to their area. I loved those people and got along very well with them. I still have two baskets woven for me by a wonderful Indian woman.

Another wonderful memory I have is of Ron Franklin, an old prospector who lived in Boston Bar. He became a good friend. He had wonderful stories about exploring the Wild West Mountains, forests and wilderness of British Columbia. He taught me how to fish in the Fraser River and once I was lucky to catch a medium sized salmon, which we had for lunch after making a fire (again taught to me by Ron). It was heaven. Ron gave me an old Indian wooden eating bowl and two Argillite small black totem poles, which he had obtained in Northern British Columbia. These items are very precious to me.

People in town knew where I lived because my office was in my house. This had a downside. A few times, I was awakened in the middle of the night by patients. Once, an Indian woman rang the doorbell about two in the morning. I opened the door. She stepped inside and could not speak. She pointed to her jaw. She had yawned and her jaw opened and got stuck. There she stood with her mouth wide open. I had not dealt with that situation before but I was lucky. With a certain pull, her jaw clicked back in place. I also had my share trying to treat sick or injured cats and dogs brought to me, and once a sick bird in a cage was presented to me. Imagine the liability if this had been in the United States. Did I mention that my annual premium for malpractice in Canada only cost $25.00 a year?

My View of History

As you know, there is fairly strong evidence that the American Indians originated from Asia and came here via Alaska about 50,000 years ago. There is also strong evidence that some Caucasian people were here prior to the Indians.

Some will remember that in the 1990's a skull (perhaps a skeleton) of a clear Caucasian man was found by a riverside in Washington State. Anthropologists called him "Kennewick man". The site where this man was found, one would expect to be "holy ground" for the scientists to further explore.

Guess what happened? President Clinton ordered the site to be completely bulldozed over and eliminated. Why? Because according to political correctness the Indians were and always will be the first and original people in North America.

Last year I attended a meeting of scientists in Las Vegas discussing nations and populations in history in America. The lady speaker enthusiastically spoke about the American Indians in the same vein as described above. During question time I tried to tell my story about "tooth" to the speaker and the audience but I was rudely cut off as soon as she realized that something politically incorrect would be pointed out.

Lytton and St. Bartholomew's Hospital were still there to my pleasant surprise, when I was able to make a nostalgic visit to Canada in 2001.

CHAPTER VII
British Columbia's Sasquatch
and the Canadian Arctic

Most people have heard of "Bigfoot" or "The Snowman" in the western U.S. and India. These stories are considered folklore or fables but I like to share what I heard while living in B.C.'s mountains, forests and rivers. First, I heard the story of something, which occurred in the late 1800,'s in the same area where I worked. It took place on the road South of Boston Bar towards Hope.

A group of trappers spotted a smallish sized animal or human walking on its two feet. They captured it and described it to be the size of an eleven to twelve year old girl. It was hairy and otherwise very human like. The story says that she was taken to Vancouver but I could not find what happened to her after that.

Another story tells that not long ago, about the time I was there, a motorist driving his car north of Lytton saw a large "human" standing on the middle of the highway. The motorist insists that it was not a bear and not a human. He got scared and slowed down. After a while the "animal" stepped away and disappeared in the forest.

Although most of these stories may not be totally based on reality, there are some aspects that makes one wonder that maybe something is going on. There is no doubt that thousands of very large foot steps have been found in America's wild northwest. There is of course the film (made by Mr. Patterson I believe) in the western U.S. which lasts about ten to fifteen seconds, showing a large, "hairy human" walking in a forest.

I would like to relate two more stories on this subject, which happened close to Lytton. The country on the west side of the Fraser River is far less populated and wild than the east side. An Indian woman living in a mobile home insists that a large Sasquatch shook her home and she saw him looking through the window. She was terrified but she survived.

A trapper/hunter had crawled in his sleeping bag for the night and was fast asleep when suddenly, he felt that someone picked the sleeping bag up with him inside. He was carried some distance and when he was put on the ground, he found himself in the company of a Sasquatch family--two large parents and two kids. The man insists that he was kept prisoner for several days and finally managed to escape and while shaking with fear was able to make it back to civilization.

These stories were told to me by the local Indians more than once. Perhaps some time in the future the truth will be revealed.

Life and science are interesting and fascinating.

Take astronomy. The latest theory about the universe, as we write this, is of course that the "Big Bang" is the beginning of everything, which of course is not very helpful for the evolutionists, because who let the big bang occur? And for what purpose? The other latest thinking is that all objects that we see as three dimensional are actually two dimensional holograms at the edge of space. I find it very hard to follow this.

Other astronomers say that the "Big Bang" is still expanding but that gravitational power pulls materials together, which means that the whole universe will ultimately collapse together into one tiny mass. I sure hope it doesn't happen during my lifetime.

After I left Lytton I went back to Vancouver where I took a residency in Anesthesiology, which was followed by many locum tenens assignments (taking the place of a doctor who takes a vacation). That means seeing his patients in his office, making rounds in the hospital, covering the emergency room, doing surgery and delivering babies. I spent a lot of time doing this in Port Alberni, Vancouver Island, which was a delightful small town, located in the middle of Vancouver Island.

In 1972-'73 I was asked to do a locum tenens in Inuvik, which is a Canadian town, located on the Arctic Ocean, just a few miles from the Alaskan border. This was quite an experience. Inuvik was something like Star Wars. If you entered the local pub or gathering place you would find many very weird looking people with long hair and beards, huge arctic clothing or uniforms. There were the local Indians,

Eskimos, Canadian military and oil people.

Working in the local hospital was quite a challenge. Once a young local Indian woman was carried in like a block of ice. She had been drinking in a local bar and fell asleep outside in the snow. Her heart was still beating. We slowly thawed her out in a bathtub and after a couple of days she was discharged. I believe she only lost two toes to frostbite. Amazing!

Besides seeing regular patients in hospital beds I had to do surgery and give anesthetics. Sometimes we had to fly out in a small plane toward the North Pole and visit Eskimo villages. Sometimes we flew south and did the same thing in Indian villages. Once I had to go out on a dog sled to visit some Indian patients. What a special experience. Of course I had to obtain a special license from the College of Physicians and Surgeons of the Northwest Territories to practice in the Arctic.

CHAPTER VIII

Practicing in Richmond, B.C., A Visit to Australia and Moving to the U.S.

I had a family practice in Richmond, B.C. for about 10 years. Richmond is a suburb just south of Vancouver not too far from the U.S. border. Again, this family practice also included surgery and anesthesiology.

To set an example for the public, I started a mile run open to the public, combined with a smoking cessation program. We managed to get onto the local radio. It was a success. I hope we started some people on the road to better health. Many doctors participated in the run. Most of my doctor friends from that period are not alive anymore.

During that time I was also President of the local Cancer Society. In the mid sixties there were rumblings in the Canadian medical world that socialized medicine would be installed. The doctors were unhappy. We had meetings with leaders of the local unions to ask their advice on how to form a doctors union. Unfortunately, our union never materialized. In Saskatchewan (two provinces further west of us), the Provincial Government and Premier, who were of the Socialist Party, were introducing socialized medicine (similar to "Obamacare") in Saskatchewan. The doctors furiously opposed it and actually went on strike. They closed their offices, but kept all hospital emergency rooms operating. They took turns around the clock so that all urgent medical problems would be taken care off. An outrage erupted amongst the public, many of whom undoubtedly had gone on strike sometime in their lives.

"How dare these evil doctors "abandon" their patients. That is absolutely terrible. They don't care about us and anyway they are all rich and spend even more time on the golf course than they usually do. What evil people they are."

The outcry was so strong that the doctors had to open their offices again. This is, to my knowledge, the only time in history that doctors went on strike.

Canada eventually instituted socialized medicine. It led to a deterioration of the quality of medical care. Many Canadians come to the U.S. for high quality medical care. I left Europe for Canada in the 1950's because of socialized medicine. Now I would leave Canada for the same reason.

Sometime in the 1970's I took a little time off to visit my brother and my sister in Australia. It was wonderful to see each other after so many years.

While I was there I applied for a license to practice in the state of New South Wales, which I was able to obtain. Then I heard that a doctor some 100 miles from Sidney in a small desert town wanted to take a few weeks' vacation. He was looking for a locum tenens. I took the job, lived in the doctor's house and worked in the local hospital.

A desert practice was new to me, especially when I was called out to see someone in the hot, lonely desert. Nevertheless, I managed and even enjoyed it.

In 1973, I decided to move to the U.S. It was sad, in a way, because British Columbia is such a wonderful province with indescribable beautiful nature. I also had to move further away from my two children. I have such beautiful memories going on vacation with them to Osprey Lake and other wonderful places.

Lordsburg, New Mexico is a small town in the Southwestern part of the state. It is located off interstate 10. The town had only one doctor, who was leaving. I was contacted and asked to move to Lordsburg. I went down first to check things out and went to Santa Fe, New Mexico's capital, to present myself to the State Board of Medical Examiners. I had a nice interview with the President of the Board and was issued a license for the state based on reciprocity, which was possible because of my European and Canadian credentials.

I made the big move and got settled in a small apartment in Lordsburg. I was again in the position of being the only doctor in town. Some of the local officials took me to the local immigration office and I was able to obtain my U.S. citizenship. I never regretted that decision. I love this unique country.

I enjoyed treating people, doing surgeries and delivering babies. Basically my practice went well, but the heavy load of being the only doctor, being called 24 hours a day is something one cannot bear too long. So after a couple of years, I wanted some relief and started to do locum tenens work back in Port Alberni on Vancouver Island for a few years. I enjoyed seeing and working with my old friends and colleagues for a while but it remained my intention to live and work in the U.S.

In 1976, I moved to Nevada, which has become my home. I settled in Carson City, the capital, in 1979 and had a nice practice. I lived in a historic house, two blocks from the Governor's mansion. The house had belonged to Lucy Crowell in the late 1880's. She was a secretary to the Nevada Supreme Court. I later met her daughter who was already an old woman, who told me interesting stories about her mother and the house. I love history and placed an historic plaque in the front yard in Lucy Crowell's honor.

I met the state Governor, Robert List, several times early in the morning when I went out jogging, as did he. John Wayne's last movie was shot two houses from mine, actually in between my house and the Governor's mansion.

I had a regular office practice and hospital privileges but I also went to the state prison to work half a day a week. That was an interesting experience, especially in the maximum-security section. I met very unusual people. One prisoner pulled one of his eyes out of the socket because he was angry and wanted to make a point. Another time I had a table thrown at me by an inmate, because I did not prescribe a narcotic medication, which he demanded.

In 1955 when I was doing a residency in a Victoria,

B.C. Hospital, there were several other doctors from The Netherlands and Britain working in Victoria hospitals. Many of us had played grass or field hockey back home. One Sunday we arranged an international match between Britain and The Netherlands. I was put in the center-forward position of the Dutch team. We had a lot of local immigrants coming out to watch this. By the time it started, there was a mini Olympics feeling. Holland won 1-0 and, yours truly, scored the only goal. What a glorious feeling! I wish upon everyone to have at least one such moment in his or her life.

CHAPTER IX
Final Move to Las Vegas

My final move in the early 90's was to Las Vegas. I did locum tenens work for a couple of large companies, mostly in urgent care clinics. This was interesting work when visitors from other countries came as patients and I could practice my other languages. I did New Year's nights shifts close to the strip and all kinds of unusual accident victims came in for treatment.

In late 2007 I started my own private practice in Vegas. I specialized in making house calls, mostly to older people who were not in very good shape and had difficulty leaving their homes. Not many doctors will do this and my patients were always very grateful.

My wife, who is a nurse from China (I met her in Beijing in '93), would often come with me. We also saw people in hotels who had gotten sick and we met a few famous celebrities. For privacy's sake I shall not mention their names.

As we gradually got busier we decided to open a small office, not far from our home for people who could and wanted to come to us and we still operate there today.

In March of 2010, the new Obamacare-law was introduced in the Congress. This law passed the Congress by one vote late on a Sunday night, with three Democrat votes bought through bribery.

The Republicans, as most Americans, were strongly opposed to socialized medicine. The Republican Congress leaders were interested in me as a spokesperson against this monstrous bill and invited me to Washington, D.C. I went to Washington the next day and attended several meetings. I met with the chief spokesman, Congressman Dr. Thomas Price and also with Congressman Dr. Burgess and several others. Congressman Price had started a new political movement called Physicians Council for Responsible Reform (PCRR). I was appointed to be the Nevada representative for PCRR. I stayed two days in Washington, D.C. and met many interesting people. They were interested in my experience and comments about European and Canadian socialized medicine and I was even asked to run for Congress for the state of Nevada.

At this writing, it is July 2012. President Obama just gave a speech, in which he clearly and honestly showed his strong Marxist views. He claimed that successful businessmen and entrepreneurs really were not successful because of their own talent or efforts, but were sort of "lucky" because others, and especially the government helped them.

Most of us feel that the great business success stories in America flowed from free enterprise, from brilliant people who created a great successful enterprise. No, says Mr. Obama, you were just lucky because others helped you, and in particular the government. Thank you, Mr. Obama for making it so crystal clear for us that you are a pure Marxist.

The fall of the Soviet Union in 1989, in my opinion, was just a small, temporary setback in the advancement of socialist Marxism in the Western world. Russia is just as communist now as it was before 1989. Of course, they discarded the silly, idealistic portions of Marxism, because a certain form of capitalism is more economically successful and creative than the old pure Marxism. But they kept the power structure and dictatorship of the country.

Even though several million Russians were killed under Mr. Lenin, his embalmed body still lies in state in a mausoleum in the main square of Moscow and still thousands of Russians come to pay their respects. Amazing! There are still 80 statues of Lenin around Moscow and hundreds around Russia! In the last election for president in Russia, guess who came in second place in that election? The leader of the (still official) Communist Party.

China did the same thing. About twenty years ago, the communist big bosses got together quietly and said to each other:

"Don't tell anyone outside this room but pure Marxism is for the birds. It keeps the country poor. Capitalism is the way to go-it will bring wealth to our country."

And so they did. They simply called it 'The Open Policy', as if it were a brand new idea. They allowed a certain form of free enterprise. And guess what? Business in China is booming and they are getting rich.

However, don't be fooled. A brutal, strict dictatorship is firmly in place. Thousands of people are imprisoned for the slightest indiscretions. Multiple people are being executed. All this is well hidden and reporters or foreigners have zero access to the details. Free speech? Ha! Are you kidding? Freedom of religion? You can be a Christian in China but only if you follow the government regulations as to how you exercise your faith.

I like to mention how nice it was to live in Carson City, Nevada. I lived in the only small historic part of the city, two blocks from the Governor's mansion, which gave a special feeling. On my days off, I would run up to Lake Tahoe, spend time in a park by the lake, and then go swimming. In the winter, I would go skiing around the Northern part of the lake. I rented skis in the lodge and I occasionally saw famous Hollywood celebrities there. The lake is so beautiful and the water is so clear, thanks to strict and proper regulation. The Winter Olympics were held around Northern Lake Tahoe once. No wonder. What fantastic, gorgeous nature.

I used to travel from Carson City southward into California, through beautiful woods and along wonderful lakes! Come and visit that part of the U.S. if you haven't been there. If you are in that area, go and visit Historic Virginia City, not far from Carson City, one of the most exciting historic mining towns in the U.S. It is wonderful for those who love history.

Have you noticed that history becomes more and more important, the older you get? Unfortunately it hardly gets taught any more in our schools, and if it does, it usually is distorted.

For a brief time, I worked part time in Hawthorne, Nevada, south of Carson City and was medical director for the military base. Close to Hawthorne is the largest ammunition storage in the U.S. This covers a few square miles with all material stored under ground but thousands of small hills indicate the site. North of Hawthorne is a huge lake. I travelled alongside this lake several times. Occasionally the winds can get so powerful that, a few times, vehicles were actually pulled into the lake.

CHAPTER X
"I Have a Dream. . . "

For years, I have had thoughts about an exciting project, which I like to call The American Center for Creative Medicine. This center would be located in a beautiful mountain setting somewhere in the Western U.S. Unfortunately I am now too old to carry this out but perhaps someone will. Let me explain my vision for this project.

I meet people who could be so much happier, searching for a better purpose, who want to look better and live better than they are. I meet such people every day.

First, I am often amazed at how terrible people dress with awful looking, mismatched clothing, clashing color combinations, bad make up and ugly beards (tattoo's are a special separate subject). I would be rude to bring this up directly to my patients. I carefully mentioned hints in connection with their illness, suggesting certain changes which will make them feel better and therefore they will also medically improve.

Secondly, people come to me for medical

problems. These problems must be diagnosed and then treated so they can be cured and feel better. This would definitely include weight loss.

Thirdly, their whole lifestyle can be discussed, which may include taking up sports, joining clubs, starting to read books.

Fourthly, people sometimes do not work in the right jobs. They could potentially thrive if some expert would analyze them and pinpoint the right direction for that person to take in life.

Fifthly, cosmetic medicine might improve people's looks. An expert in that field might point out certain things that can be done by plastic and cosmetic surgery which the patient might not be aware of, but which would greatly improve the person's life.

Sixthly, a thorough series of visits with a psychologist would probably change and greatly help the patient.

Seventhly, spiritual guidance would also very much contribute to become a "better" person. The patient would decide the type of this spiritual path (Christian, Mormon etc.)

Eighth, the patient would be taught financial planning for their life now, for their children and for retirement.

My plan would cover all these items in one large facility. Patients would spend several weeks with us. Obviously, this would not be cheap, but there could be a market for this idea.

It would start with a screening process for each new visitor with a long, reassuring conversation, covering all above subjects with no holds barred. This would be followed by designing a comprehensive plan. We would have experts in every field: top physicians and diagnostic tools, including surgical procedures, psychologists, financial advisers, sports trainers, job advisors, and ministers and spiritual leaders from many denominations. In summary, our patients would come for a complete makeover and take their time to reach all their goals. Their life would totally change for the better with, in my opinion, very exciting changes for the better. Patients could come back anytime they wish or feel the need for a refresher. As stated before, this would all be expensive but I believe it would also be an enhancing factor in our society. People would be proud to be "graduates" of our clinic.

I am now an old man but, God knows, sometime, somewhere this idea could be carried out and our center would become famous. I just wanted to share these ideas with those who read this little book and then laugh or think I am crazy or perhaps think there is some validity in my ideas.

CHAPTER XI
The Meaning of Medical Practice
and my Spiritual Outlook

I'd like to finish this book with two items. Number one: What did and does medical practice mean to me and what was and is my particular interest in treating people. Number two: I wish to share my spiritual development and thoughts about life and death.

Firstly, I want to talk about what makes being a physician exciting for me. I don't wish to sound phony but I like and love people. I enjoy speaking to people because each human being is unique and interesting. My questions to them go far beyond just their medical problems. I believe that my questions are ultimately relevant and will help to establish and nourish a good doctor-patient relationship, which is so crucial, especially in family medicine. I ask them about their work, their hobbies, their relationship with their love ones, their faith and so on. I don't push too hard and my discussions with them are very much appreciated by the patient. We usually end up as friends. Some questions touch on intimate subjects, but I am very careful not to push too far. Getting to know my patients is helpful, firstly, to understand the "whole human being" and secondly, to develop a trust between us and obtain better knowledge how best to treat this person. Some people collect stamps. I collect people.

In the last thirty to forty years, I've developed a particular interest in treating pain and an urge to relieve acute and chronic pain so that people could have an amazing improvement in their quality of life. Because of this, I did a residency in the 50's in anesthesiology in Vancouver. I worked at Complete Care Medical Center for 11 years--a clinic in Las Vegas, which specialized in treating people who suffer pain from recent accidents. I even became medical director of that clinic. My interest in pain relief also led me to work at Pacific Family Clinic, another clinic, which specialized in treating people who had been involved in car and other accidents. When I started my own clinic in 2007, pain treatment became one of the major parts of the practice, especially when we made house calls to people who were debilitated and bedridden and suffering severe chronic pain. What a privilege it is for me to relieve their suffering and see a smile.

I'd like to end my life story with an overview of my spiritual development over the course of eighty plus years. As I mentioned early in this book, I was born in the South of Holland, where the people overwhelmingly were Catholic-Christians. Our family was not really Protestant, in that we didn't go to a church regularly, but you could say that we leaned that way.

I personally believe that the whole western

European civilization was based on Christ, even though the official practice and church going were considerably diminished from a few hundred years earlier. Basic goodness, courtesy, civilized behavior, decency, good laws essentially prevailed in Western Europe.

What is happening now in Europe with the very large influx of Muslims, I believe reflects a total, drastic, change in the situation. The outlook is uncertain, actually perhaps it is certain, unavoidable and scary.

In my early years in Canada my spiritual life was unchanged and a carryover from my European years but in the early 1970's it changed. I was doing locum tenens work in Port Alberni, a lovely town, located in mid Vancouver Island on the West Pacific coast. The major industry in the town was based on a huge lumber plant. The lumber industry was at that time one of the major economic enterprises of British Columbia.

One day I met an elderly English lady who lived close to Port Alberni. She was well educated and interesting. She was a minister. Her faith which was basically Christian was based on the belief that we come to this earth from a previous life. The Lord's purpose of us being born again is to use the time of our life on this earth to grow in spirit, so that when we finally die we are on a higher spiritual level than when we were born.

Some of us go through life with few problems, but some others go through severe, very difficult situations. One might say that the first group undergoes a fairly basic spiritual education, but the second group is actually privileged because they go through "Harvard" and end up on a much higher spiritual level. Often we scream and protest, "Why is this happening to me?" I believe that everything that happens to us has a purpose and that once we pass on it will be revealed to us why.

My experiences with my English friend started out fairly general and routine. Hilda, (bless her soul) believed and practiced sessions and contacts with souls/spirits, who had passed on and she also practiced 'spiritual healing'. This subject interested me very much and I participated with her to make contact with spirits and in healing some patients. One of the spirits we dealt with was the late Archbishop of Canterbury, who of course was at one time the leader of the Anglican Church in Britain.

Apart from my regular medical treatment during the early 1970's, I worked with Hilda off and on and practiced spiritual healing. The contacts we made and the positive results we achieved were encouraging to me and I could see no possible harm in what we did. Many times, she came to me with statements from the 'other side' about certain facts and conditions which were known to me alone and which I had never discussed with her.

These statements impressed me greatly and made me believe that what we did was true and genuine and proper. I was even interviewed by a local newspaper, which wrote a long article about our faith healing or spiritual healing. I believe that today in England this movement is still alive and well.

In the mid to late 1970's, when I moved to the United States, I lost contact with Hilda. I first practiced in Southern New Mexico as I discussed earlier in this book, but did not practice spiritual healing by myself.

My last spiritual journey began in about 1983. Although I was not a regular churchgoer I frequently watched Sunday morning church services on television, which made me feel good. I also began to read the Bible regularly. On one Sunday came the big moment. I watched a service by Jimmy Swaggart and joyfully gave my heart to Jesus. I was born again. (Jimmy got into some trouble later but that is not important because when he helped me to accept Christ he was an instrument of the Lord). I became a devout Christian and will be for the rest of my life. Reading the Bible told me clearly that attempts to contact spirits is not biblical and is discouraged. Yes, I know that people like Dr. Kuebler Ross have done and are doing some spectacular and remarkable things and I respect them but I have decided to follow the Bible more closely. It is such a joy, after I ask a patient if he or she is a Christian, to share our faith. I see many times how uplifting and healing this is for the patient to be able to discuss their convictions with their physician. I am a Christian by faith.

Many Americans, nowadays, ridicule Christianity.

"It is just for old ladies. The Bible is just a fairy tale, with absolutely no proof of reality".

I need no 'proof' but it is interesting that stories in the Bible over the last few decades are gradually verified by archeologists and archeological findings. Clay tablets from the early second millennium

B.C. list cities that match the names of Abraham's relatives. These include: Peleg, Serug, Nahor, Terah and Heran (Genesis 11:17.32). Genesis 11.31 tells us that Abraham emigrated with his family from "UR of the Chaldeans". The ruins of this city were discovered in South Eastern Iraq. Abraham's father, Terah, died in the city of Heran which now lies in Turkey; and Abraham's wife, Sarah died in Hebron, one of the oldest still inhabited cities of the middle East (Genesis 11:32;23:2).

Earlier, I mentioned that Isaiah prophesied the coming and life of Christ 750 years before it happened and that other prophets did the same. What are the odds for such prophesies to come true, going by the law of averages? Pretty impressive! I predict that in the coming years more and more archeological proof will be discovered to verify the Bible, but again, for me far more important is being born again after giving my heart to Christ.

CHAPTER XII
Some Additional
Thoughts and Pearls

1) We are witnessing the most brutal irony in history. In about 200 B.C. King Cyrus the Great of Persia helped the Israelis, who were in Babylon and had suffered many years of captivity in the Assyrian Empire and then under King Belshazzar of Babylonia. Cyrus brought the Israelis back to their home in Israel and even helped them to rebuild Solomon's temple. Today, the same country, Iran, plans to wipe all Jews off the face of the earth.

2) The planets in our solar system keep nicely rotating in a precise circle around the sun. Just a moment. Precise, is not quite the right term. Jupiter's circle around the sun is not absolutely constant. Over many years the circle changes a little. Therefore the much smaller planet Mercury is also thrown a little off balance. Astronomers predict that in the long run a near-collision or collision with Earth will happen which would result in a huge burn-up of both planets.

The above was written in June '80 in Holland sent to the Editor of "The Telegraaf" but not printed.

Visiting from the United States in this wonderful country of my birth after an absence of 26 years, one goes through a great number of cultural shocks and amazement at so many changes, and certainly not all for the worse.

On this occasion I should like to comment on the Paralympics, the Olympic Games for the Disabled to be held in Arnhem this summer. Interestingly South African white and black disabled athletes will be banned from these games; however Polish, Tsjech and Yugoslavian participants will be allowed. The only reason the Soviet Union does not participate is because it claims that it has no disabled athletes.

Generally speaking, the same people who advocate for Dutch athletes to go to Moscow because politics should play no role in international sports are defending this highly political decision. In Marxist dialectic philosophy, it is of course quite normal and very allowable to think in double standards.

For the uninformed: Dialectics is the Art of holding up a black object and then talking so long and so cleverly that you convince the audience that the object is in fact white.

For instance, the American Communist Party's official stand is against nuclear energy for the United States and it advocates (with people like Jane Fonda carrying the banner) the closure of existing and the stopping of future nuclear power plants in the USA, however this same Communist Party is for nuclear energy in the Soviet Union.

If it is true that human rights is the issue (as the anti-South Africa people claim) to decide on

118

the participation of countries in the Olympics then surely to God the first nations to ban would be all communist countries where human rights (including racial rights) have been, are, and will be violated on a scale ten times greater than in South Africa, which allows formation of all political parties, which has a virtual unlimited freedom of the press and a standard of living for all races which is much higher than in any communist country. It not only allows all its citizens to leave the country at will but has a problem with people wanting to come into South Africa because of the higher standard of living. Our anti South Africa theorists won't mention this. How different

is reality often from theory! People are not stupid. "They vote with their feet" as we clearly see in Vietnam, Cambodia and Cuba.

In the Soviet Union alone at least 26 million people have been killed for political reasons and today hundreds of thousands are political prisoners in the Gulags. There is no freedom of the press no free movement across borders, no freedom of speech whatsoever. There is one and only one political party and no opposition, the standard of living is low and there is political persecution and racial discrimination of Jews.

One would think therefore that the people who are so concerned about some violation of human rights in South Africa would go out of their minds with concerns over the far and far worse violations of human rights in Communist countries. They ought to scream and yell at the top of their voices with outrage over so much human rights violation.

But no, there is a strange and eerie silence from that segment of concerned citizens when it comes to the Soviet Union and its friends. They, in fact, see no problem in warm and friendly associations in sports and otherwise with these representatives of international gangster nations.

This strange phenomenon of intellectual dishonesty amongst "respectable" Western citizens is ominous and is not confined to Europe. North America has its share of the same kind of "thinkers". Moscow must be delighted and the vodka must be flowing freely at the parties to celebrate such success.

I think it is obvious that the greatest dangers facing the West do not come from Russian guns and tanks but from our own inner decay as is evident from the thinking of our own good people.

This may very well be the main cause for the imminent and apparent beginning of the end of our Western Civilization.

Chapter XIII
The State of the Union

I would like to talk about some experiences I had as a student in Amsterdam. At the university, we had different groups of students: a Catholic group, Protestant, Socialist and Communist. We debated furiously. I found myself initially drawn to socialism, because it seemed fair that those who were not too well off should be helped by those who were. Later on, over the next few years, I moved gradually more rightward and became a conservative.

We had hot debates with the Communist students in Amsterdam. Stalin had a hundred year plan to conquer the western world without firing a shot. This plan is being carried out as we speak. Communism hates free enterprise and capitalism (just read "Das Kapital" by Karl Marx). Our communist friends told us clearly what Moscow's instructions to them were, "Go into the media and into education." Why? Because once you have a good position in a newspaper, TV etc. you give everything a liberal-socialist, Marxist slant. Once you are a teacher push the socialist, Marxist line. Then look at today. Aren't they succeeding? American education puts an emphasis on political correctness, sex, (preferably abnormal sex) and socialism-Marxism. Geography and history are practically out the window.

Stalin, who died in 1952, is jumping out of his grave with excitement. I don't think he ever dreamed of so much success in fifty years.

At the same time in today's schools, Christianity, conservatism and individual freedom are ridiculed and criticized. From my conversations with the Soviet military and later with Communist students in Amsterdam, I learned about their training, teaching and modus operandi. First of all, they are well schooled in Karl Marx's books and secondly they learn from the communist bible Dialectic Materialism.

What this teaches them, for instance, is the great art of clever speaking. One can speak to an audience, hold up a black object and talk so clever that half an hour later the audience is absolutely convinced that the object is white.

The concept of lying is very different for a well-trained Marxist. They make a statement and a few days later while somewhere else they make an opposite statement. To us that is ludicrous and deceitful. To them it is very different. There is only one requirement. "If at the moment you make a statement it supports and advances the cause of Marxism/Communism, making the statement is moral."

People are astonished by Mr. Obama's statements, which often are one hundred percent the opposite of what he said years before. From his Marxist's standpoint that is totally okay. Does one doubt his

Marxist philosophy? As a physician, I constantly have to make a diagnosis. A diagnosis is made after a good history and physical assessment of the patient.

Let us take a good history of our President. Both of his parents were Marxist/Communist. All his friends and teachers were strong Marxists and many hate America. Some even carried out terrorists acts, such as trying to bomb the Pentagon. Mr. Obama stated on TV that his Muslim faith (Oh, ha, ha, of course, I mean Christian faith) was very important to him. He stated that he visited all 57 states of the U.S. Doesn't the Arab league have 57 members internationally?

He faithfully attended a Christian church where he listened to his friend, Reverend Wright, who served as pastor at Obama's wedding. He sat in Wright's church for twenty years while Mr. Wright clearly stated that he hated America, whites and Jews. Now Mr. Obama claims that he didn't remember these rants and statements coming from Mr. Wright. Reverend Wright bases his theology on "Black Liberation Theology" which includes hatred of whites. To include this in the greater concept of Christianity is a far stretch. There are two possibilities. Either Mr. Obama did not notice, in which case he would be far too dumb to be President, or he lied. Take your pick.

Mr. Obama's college and many other records will never be made public. Once one realizes that we are dealing with a pure, un-adulterated Marxist, everything happening in the U.S. during his Presidency makes complete sense. As a good Marxist you would hate the U.S. as it is, because in an ideal Marxist setting free enterprise and capitalism are evil and have to be eliminated. The government is superior, knows better what is good for you and has to be in charge of everything.

Many people ask, "Why is he doing this? Why is he doing that?" Of course he is doing those things. He is systematically trying to nationalize all activities in the U.S.--the auto industry, the financial world, education, healthcare etc.. Once all free enterprise is removed, the government will run the whole country telling everyone what they can and cannot do. He is raising a "workers' paradise," purely according to Karl Marx. If he is reelected and manages to have a similar successor, all our freedoms will be gone and we become slaves.

Barack Obama is on this mission! The result will be that we are all equally poor but there will be a super class of Marxist leaders (as there was in the Soviet Union) who have huge incomes, beautiful mansions, superior medical care in their special private hospitals. They deserve this because only they know what is good for the rest of us (because we are too stupid to know for ourselves). They benevolently will dish out to us some goodies. This is the future of the United States of America, but actually, it will be worse than the above picture. We will not just have communism or Castroism; we will have "Communism-plus." What is the plus? We will have Communism, plus political correctness, plus liberalism.

What do I mean by that? First of all pure Marxism will be implemented far more rigidly than in the old Soviet Union. I say this because in general the U.S. government is far more regulated than any country in history. Every breath has to be recorded and tens of thousands of inspectors will make sure that you did precisely as the government told you, or else. Political correctness? Do you think that homosexuality was pushed as hard in the Soviet Union as it is here? Do you think that in education the most important goal was to make sure that Johnny's self-esteem would not be hurt? That would be laughed at in the Soviet Union.

What about same sex marriage? Yes, it is only "fair" that two men who love each other should have the status of marriage. Of course. Next, a 40-year-old man walks in with a 10-year-old boy: "We love each other. We want to get married. How can you be so unfair and narrow-minded to deny us to be married?" Next, a woman walks in with a shepherd dog saying the same thing. What a wonderful world we are turning into-a politically correct, monstrous police state.

Many people in our country have no clue of the direction we are going. A clever ultra liberal candidate can easily persuade them with, "Those greedy capitalists take your money but if you elect me I will take that money back from them and give it all to you."

Wow! Enormous applause. Result? Millions of young voters for Obama.

The truth will never be taught by our Marxist leaning teachers to our students. For instance, a discussion about wealth. According to liberal teachings, wealth is found. Picture a bunch of orange trees filled with oranges. People like to eat those oranges. Liberal teaching is that the people with the strongest legs run to the orchard, get there first and therefore get most of the oranges, whereas those with weaker legs get very little. That is not fair. Truthful teaching would point out that wealth is not found, those who happen to have sharp brains and strong motivation create it. These people start businesses and provide jobs for millions of others. Therefore, everyone gains.

Question: Should those who create wealth not be able to keep it? If I make something, isn't it mine? Of course it is, especially because of my efforts and my creation I help others to gain wealth. No, in the liberal philosophy if you become wealthy you are guilty of being greedy. Yes but I didn't take it away from others? It didn't exist before I created it. That doesn't matter. They will take my wealth and distribute it to others. Well in that case, I will stop producing wealth or I'll go to another country, where the government will not rob me blind.

We wonder why our economy is so bad now. It is so logical, so simple. The other day I was at a business, waiting my turn. A gentleman walked in wearing a T-shirt saying, "Legal immigrant from Cuba." We started talking about Castro's Cuba. He immediately said that under President Obama we are entering the same hell as Cuba and that most Americans have no clue as to what is happening.

I told him that I agreed with him one hundred percent and had wide international experience coming from Europe, World War II etc. We agreed that we should pray for America to wake up.

I'd like to touch on global warming and

environmentalism. I remember in 1970 the world renowned (and respected) scientist Dr. Ehrlich making a big speech about the new ice age just around the corner. In the same period another scientist (or was it Ehrlich) predicted that the world would run out of food within a few years. This same scientist is still highly respected in many circles of the world. Others claim that the world is getting warmer and that it is our fault. A few years ago, National Geographic ran an article about Mars. One observation was that Mars was also getting warmer, just like the Earth, over the last few years. Well, why would that be? What have Earth and Mars in common? Think very hard. Oh, they are both planets and receive their light from the Sun. So, if the Sun at certain times is more active and there are more sun explosions etc. the heat from the Sun, can be felt as increased heat by all these planets. Wow! What an amazing thought.

Actually, a child could have told you that. You don't believe that? About two years ago, our whole family was sitting in our backyard enjoying the beautiful summer evening. One of us said, "Look at that beautiful bright star."

Within seconds, a little voice from behind us said, "No, that is not a star. That is a planet."

I had to pinch myself to make sure I heard that, because it came from my 3-year-old grandson. He was right. It was Venus. He was smarter than Dr. Ehrlich, unless Dr. Ehrlich is just as smart as or smarter than he is but says what he says, knowing that it is untrue, but says it anyway. In other words, might he have an ulterior purpose to say what he says? Maybe his friends do the same thing and came up with certain theories, which are untrue. Well, what a shocking thought.

Actually, that is happening. Do you remember the exposure of certain scientists at the Anglia University in Britain, who came with conclusions about global warming, which were based on false, made up facts and assumptions? Do you remember Al Gore telling us that the North Pole polar bears were dying out and then it turned out that their numbers were actually increasing?

The truth consists of a mixture of good and bad things. Many people are concerned that nature, animals, parks, plants may be under threat of extinction from human interference and activity. I totally agree with that. I love all nature, the beautiful creation of fantastic animals, birds, butterflies, insects, flowers, trees etc. By all means, let us treat them with respect and love and let us try to preserve them, but let us be reasonable. Let us not punish a man who cleans up a pool of water on his property and slap him with a $100,000-fine.

A couple of years ago a large portion of Southern California was declared a special water zone, because of a tiny fish. A few million people were punished by not being able to use any more water in that part of California. This involved many farmers and wiped out many businesses. Surely, some other, more moderate solution could have saved that little fish.

This form of government torture is almost evil. It fits in with the liberal tendency to control our lives ultimately completely and this is of course the ideal liberal goal. "You don't know what is good for you. "You are too stupid and irresponsible. The government knows much better what is right and wrong for you than you know yourself."

This attitude, this program if fully implemented, will ultimately lead to a total socialist, Marxist dictatorship. Hence, more and more regulations are put upon us. This is understandable because government has been growing like a cancer, like a very bad virus. It is practically unstoppable.

Thousands of federal bureaucrats have the assignment to justify their incomes. They constantly have to come up with new regulations, which they show to their bosses and are then patted on the back. This country is being regulated to death. What do we do about that? It will be extremely difficult to stop this evil process, and can only be done at great political costs. It will take a very strong president to turn this around. Ronald Reagan was such a man.

God help us all. The obsession of wanting to run us all is, of course, pure Marxism and the world has seen a few examples of that. "We will take the wealth of those greedy capitalists (which they stole from you people) and distribute it to you nice and equally." The result is a ruling class, like in the Soviet Union and Cuba, which has the nicest homes, the highest income, the finest healthcare in their own special hospital etc., because since they are the leaders they surely deserve everything they got. After all, aren't they taking care of us and distribute the goodies to us, like throwing food at zoo animals?

Health care is now on the front burner. At the time

of this writing, the Supreme Court of the U.S. has just passed a final verdict on Obamacare. Justice Roberts declared the mandate (the money you must pay to the government if you don't want to be penalized) constitutional, as long as it is called a "tax."

As a physician, I have strong feelings about this. I left the Netherlands in 1954 to get away from socialized medicine, and went to Canada. I moved to the U.S. in 1974 when Canada introduced socialized national healthcare.

A physician is an independent professional. The practice of medicine is an art, (even though it is based on science). Should the government tell an artist what colors, what brushes, what canvas to use? It would lead to the destruction of art. If you want to destroy medicine, socialize it.

What is wrong with the Republican leadership? President Ford nominated Justice Stevens to the Supreme Court, who turned out not to be much of a conservative. President Bush nominated Mr. Soeter to the Supreme Court, who turned one hundred and eighty degrees and turned out to be a flaming liberal. Did President George W. Bush make the same stupid mistake, appointing a liberal, Mr. Roberts, to the Supreme Court?

"We want to compromise, we want to reach across the aisle." Yes. Go ahead and do that. They will grab your hand and pull you right over to the liberal side. Have you ever seen a liberal reach across the aisle? Of course not. It is all one sided. They are laughing about our stupidity.

President Eisenhower appointed Justice Warren

to the Supreme Court. Later on Mr. Eisenhower said, "That is the stupidest thing I ever did."

There are some people who think that Justice Robert's decision is so cleverly complicated that it will result in Obamacare being defeated and eliminated, and that he is, in fact, a good (and very sharp and clever) conservative. I am praying hard, because if not, if Obamacare gets fully implemented, the finest and by far the best medical care in the world will be destroyed and like in the Soviet Union, doctors will be mostly mediocre intelligent women, treated like maids and paid like maids.

If I go to an attorney with a problem, he listens to my case and says, "Sure, I'll be happy to take your case, just make an appointment for next week and bring a check for $2,000 to start."

Now let us switch to medicine. A woman comes in and has Medicare or some other insurance. I spend at least half an hour with her. Of course, she pays nothing out of her pocket. I may be very lucky and get forty deductible from the patient. Then my charge goes to my biller. About a month later, I may receive a check for $56.00. I also may get nothing. Almost daily, I get a letter from an insurance company saying, "You saw Mrs. so and so on such and such a date and used code number so and so. Your final payment is $0.00, because code such and such was not completed or does not apply in this case." I let my staff get on the phone and try to collect, but that is useless because of the time involved waiting on the phone, and usually does not result in payment. Could I try to bill Mrs. X for her visit? If she happens to have Medicare, it would be against the law for her to pay me and for me to receive her money. Anyway, patients really don't want to pay a doctor, because it does not get anything nice. You pay for your food, entertainment, your liquor, but you don't pay a doctor. "Some insurance or some other entity will pay him. Anyway all doctors are wealthy and greedy and spend several days a week on the golf course." I know that I am generalizing, which is not quite fair, but I have seen the same line of thinking in Europe and Canada and the U.S. has become infected with this attitude in the last twenty to thirty years.

All this will result in thousands of doctors leaving the profession, retiring, or going into real estate. You hear this mentioned on T.V. but by far not often enough. Doctors will also strongly discourage their children to go into medicine. In the future, there will be "providers." They will be Physicians Assistants and Family nurse practitioners or some person with a medical degree from Bangladesh whose English is not easily understood. The wait at Emergency Rooms and urgent care clinics will be longer and when you are finally seen, the "doctor" will spend a few minutes with you at most. The public anger and protests will be loud and substantial, but it will all be in vain, because it will be too late. You asked for it; you said you wanted "free medical care, available for everyone."

There is now a prevailing philosophy "If I am born in the U.S. I am entitled to food, housing, medical care." That simply means that your neighbor, who is 35, works for a construction company and gets on the freeway early in the morning with his lunch bucket after kissing his wife and three children good bye, will be the one whose tax money will pay for all your entitlements, while you can stay at home all day watching T.V.

It is now getting so preposterous that a young unmarried woman, who sleeps around at random, is now "entitled" to get her birth control medication, paid for by her neighbors, who have a hard time with their money and are living very frugally. Now her sex life has to be financed by others, who may not have any sexual enjoyment at all!

How deep have we sunk in liberal idiocy? These are huge issues. This should be front-page news. The T.V. tells us about a "bully" who hit another child, about little Mary, who lost her teddy bear, but the above problems are hardly mentioned. I rarely see a doctor interviewed to discuss issues and problems in the medical world.

I wish to honor my brother Robert by talking about him. As mentioned before we were both in the Dutch Underground Forces in WWII and he was beside me when we were in the frontline, in October 1944 to spy on German positions. Suddenly, grenades started to fall around us and I was wounded. My brother saved my life and managed to take me to a hospital.

Robert, after the war, went to the University of Wageningen where he became an agricultural engineer. He was married in approximately 1954 and immigrated to Australia, where he became a scientist for the famous and illustrious CSIRO, a government scientific organization and of course, as a government university connected scientist, he became a liberal.

He couldn't be more apart from me as a "born-again" Christian. I always honored his viewpoints and we had some interesting discussions. While he was in Australia, I was in Canada and the U.S., and over more than twenty years, we did not see each other very often.

We talked about evolution. I pointed out that for evolution to be true, the mathematical odds would be the same as a storm blowing through a junkyard and putting a 747-jet plane together or to throw the dices at a crap-table and come up with two sixes one hundred thousand times in a row. Some years ago this was already pointed out by non-evolutionists who said that for evolution to have created all life a few atoms have to bounce together and accidentally put an amino acid together. Not only that, it would have to be a left-handed amino acid. Then you need a bunch of amino acids "accidentally" to form a protein. Then many proteins bouncing together have to form a cell (by the way, there is more information in a living cell than there is in Encyclopedia Britannica!). Then you have to believe that billions, if not trillions of cells have to form an organism, a living being. As stated before, years ago some non-evolutionists pointed out the absurdity of these happenings. Now we live in a time that with high mathematics and computers it can be stated that the above evolution theory is absolutely impossible. Hence, there is now, among top scientists the theory of "Intelligent Design" which concludes that only a superior artist/intellect could have produced life as we see it.

In addition, I like to pose the question: If evolution caused all life 'by accident', how could it have caused love, feelings? Is Beethoven's Fifth Symphony the result of some atoms bouncing together? I do believe that a Creator created life but that it is quite possible that from time to time some anatomical features in birds or other animals changed over millions of years to adapt the animal to certain environmental changes.

I also pointed out to my brother that if you ask a stockbroker what he thinks a Coca Cola share will be tomorrow, he couldn't tell you. However, the prophet Isaiah predicted 750 years before Jesus' birth that there would be a Jesus and also several details of his life. In addition, other prophets predicted the same details. As the years go by archeologists and anthropologists confirm more and more details about the facts mentioned in the bible.

In spite of our discussions, Robert remained a liberal until his death 1 ½ years ago from chronic lung disease. I want to say that I always loved him and respected him both as brother and as a scientist. He was regarded as a top agronomist in the university world and published a large number of important articles. He spent a long time in Indonesia and Vietnam where the CSIRO sent him for research. May God bless his soul. He was a good and honorable man.

Anyway, I cannot accept evolution as a total explanation of life. When I look at my beautiful 5-year-old grandson, I am in awe of the immense complexities of putting such an amazing package together.

CHAPTER XIV
A (Possibly) True Story

Some millions of miles from the Earth sits a planet, which is not unlike ours. It is called Joshua, it circles around its sun, receiving light, and therefore it has life--human like life. The people of Joshua are intelligent and their science has progressed so far, that they are ready for spaceflight. Not just orbital flight, but deep, distant spaceflight. Their astronomers long ago determined that far away there is another small planetary system and one of the planets probably supports human life. You guessed it. They chose Earth.

Their technical skills are so far developed that a long trip is possible--a trip of 100 years or more. Volunteers were hard to find. The people involved would never see home again. The journey will take generations. They are able to find fifty crazy people--twenty-five healthy, intelligent men and twenty-five intelligent women who don't mind getting married and procreating while on a long, tedious, trip into space.

The preparation for this trip is mind-boggling.

How do they manage to make sure they will have food, many, many years from now? How do they keep their astronauts from going berserk, keep them motivated, educated, psychologically and emotionally stable? What to do with the bodies of people who die during the journey?

The Joshuans put it all together. On a National Holiday of Joshua, the spacecraft called Madison launched with fifty passengers. Millions of Joshuan's watched either in person or by broadcast. Emotions run high and deep. Citizens openly cry and celebrate. They are on their way.

The carefully chosen volunteers do well because of their thorough preparations. The leadership on board is strong and able to keep a harmonious, disciplined atmosphere.

Years and years go by. Madison holds up well through many decades. Near collisions with other space material was avoided because of their superb technology.

They near the solar system of Earth. The pilots make contact with Earth officials, who are surprised and not sure what to think. Something new is happening and everyone on Earth is excited.

They find a way to communicate with the Earthlings through their science, computer, and math. Madison is being monitored by Earth's scientists now. They arrange the day of landing. Both parties agree on California's Vandenberg's airstrip.

All people now on board the Madison have never seen Joshua. They were born after the departure.

The world press goes crazy when they land. Earth

leader, President Noah is present. By coordinating with Earth's specialists, Madison lands perfectly.

Madison's leaders exit the vehicle and greet President Noah and other Earth leaders.

The Joshuans marvel as they take in the sights of Earth. Many things confound them. They see land covered with a green color and tall poles with side branches covered with little pieces of green. They see smaller green sticks with beautiful, multicolored heads. They see some beings flying around in all shapes and sizes, most of them with beautiful colors.

With express amazement and awe, they ask their hosts, "What are all these gorgeous things we see?"

"Oh, we call those trees, grass, flowers and birds."

"How do you get these things?" they ask.

"Well, they were always here, maybe for millions of years, as far as we can determine"

One of the leading and most educated Joshuans comes forward and says, "That is amazing. The surface of Joshua, other than some space for housing and roads, is completely covered with windmills and solar panels to produce our energy. Why don't you have that? Where do you get your energy from?" He turned to President Noah. "Over the centuries, we needed more and more energy. We had no choice but to build more and more solar panels and windmills. We could not get energy from anywhere else. In our history books, I read that thousands of years ago, there were such things as plant and animal life on Joshua but all that was given up in order to have energy for our daily lives and activities. How do the people on Earth manage to have active, modern lives?"

President Noah shook his head. "We manage to get our energy from other sources. We dig in the Earth deep enough, to find a liquid we call oil. We also found what we call gas. These two substances have been giving us all the energy we need for thousands of years. In addition, our chemical specialists have been studying molecules and atoms and have discovered what we call atomic energy. Could your planet have similar recourses underground?"

The Joshuan stood dumb founded. "I am amazed at your ingenuity. I will communicate with my colleagues back home and tell them what I have seen and learned. Perhaps there is still some hope for us. If we could perhaps take some samples and seeds back home to try and change our environment, maybe we could share these beautiful things, which you call nature, even though it would take generations to achieve."

President Noah was deeply moved. "Of course, we will help you all we can. Many years ago, there was a worldwide movement here on Earth, which pushed an idea called climate change. These people were adamant that we stop using oil, gas and atomic energy. Instead, we should get our energy only from sunshine and wind. They were very persuasive and almost convinced the majority that they were right. Thank God, we were able to stop their movement and still obtain most of our energy from oil, gas and coal. It was a close call and we almost lost the battle. But we won. We can produce all the energy we need on this earth and still enjoy our wonderful, beautiful, colorful nature."

President Noah gathered all his appropriate scientists and experts. They gathered samples and information together for the Joshuans.

An emotional and historic farewell took place when the Joshuans boarded Madison . Earth would never be the same. Most earthlings agreed that we are extremely blessed to be surrounded by God's creations. They give them the physical, emotional and spiritual enjoyment of the immense beauties of all nature's products.

Earth's Christians prayed very hard for the Joshuans to enjoy the same, even if it would be in the far future.

From
My Diary
in World War II

ADDENDUM I
My World War II Diary

I will quote some entries from my diary, which I kept from 1942 to 1944. Most of the material is personal but I thought that it would be nice to share some of this historic material.

March 1 '42: Attack on Java by the Japanese. Half of 40 Dutch ships were sunk. They landed at 3 points: At Bambam, near Indramajor and near Rembang. Two of the 3 Dutch cruisers were sunk: The "De Ruiter" and the "Java". Oil Installations of Tjepoe on Java were destroyed by the Dutch Military.

March 2 '42: Heavy fighting on Java.

March 3 '42: The Duke of Aosta, the chief commander of the Italian troops in Ethiopia died in captivity. Dutch troops fighting hard against the Japanese on Java. The Dutch General Ten Poorten is appointed to be commander of all allied troops on Java (Dutch, English and American).

March 4 '42: The RAF (British Air Force) announced that it will bomb factories in the occupied countries, which work for Germany. The Renault factories near Paris were bombed.

March 5 '42: Batavia, Indonesia's capital falls to the Japanese.

March 8 '42: Java's last holdout in Bandung falls to the Japanese; Roosevelt signs a war budget of $32 billion.

March 11 '42: Large supplies of war material from the U.S arrive in Australia.

March 12 '42: New contingents of American troops arrive on the Island of Curacao and in Surinam (both Dutch colonies in South America to strengthen the defense of the territories). Apparently there is still some fighting on East Java by Dutch and Australian troops.

March 13 '42: The Australian and American Air forces bomb Japanese ships which appear north of Australia. They want to make sure that Australia does not get invaded.

March 16 '42: General McArthur will command all forces, which defend Australia.

March 17 '42: The Dutch pilot Smirnoff flew a number of people from Indonesia to Australia. This plane was shot at repeatedly by the Japanese Air Force but Smirnoff, although badly wounded, managed to complete his flight and land in Australia.

March 19 '42: In Burma a Chinese Army fights under the command of an American General.

March 21' 42: The German General Rommel is preparing an attack on the British forces in Libya.

March 22 '42: A Russian Marshall is preparing a strong defense against the Germans. He has 122 divisions ready to fight and has a lot of American supplies.

March 23 '42: New contingents of Canadian, Polish and Dutch troops have arrived in England from Canada.

March 30 '42: British Sir Stafford Cripps was assigned by the British Government to go to India. His job is to stimulate the Indians to help Britain with the war effort and he promises India complete independence after the war.

April 1 '42: A British convoy on its way to the Soviet Union, north of Norway, was attacked by German destroyers. The cruiser "Trinidad" attacked the German warships and sank a German destroyer. Somewhat later near Murmansk British U boats with cooperation of the Soviet Navy attacked the German Navy and severely damaged 3 German U boats. As a result the Allied convoys reach Murmansk.

April 2 '42: The United States reports that so far 25 German U boats have been destroyed.

147

April 3 '42: Dutch and Australian troops are still fighting the Japanese on Java.

April 4 '42: Since the start of the war on December 6 '41 the United States is in the process of building 17 battleships, 17 aircraft carriers, 17 heavy cruisers, 40 light cruisers and 120 destroyers. In '42 America will build 65,000 planes. In 1943, 125,000!

April 7 '42: 300 British RAF bombers attacked French factories which manufacture important airplanes parts. They did considerable damage. German General Rommel and his troops are very active and seem to be preparing a big operation.

April 9 '42: In Holland "smokes" are being rationed. Men 18 years or older will receive a "tobacco-card" which will issue them 40 cigarettes or 10 cigars per week. Women 24 years or older will receive a card for 40 cigarettes for 4 weeks. Younger people will get special rations which will give them candies.

April 10 '42: The Japanese Air Force has been attacking Ceylon (now called Sri Lanka) and lost about 100 planes!

April 13 '42: No German planes appeared over England for more than a day. It appears that this may be the end of German bombardments over England. The Germans need their Air Force over Russia much more than on the West front.

April 14 '42: General Von Rundstedt has been put in charge of all 20 German Divisions in France by Hitler. There are rumors of a possible Allied invasion on the French Coast.

April 16 '42: 13 American heavy bombers flew on a special assignment by General McArthur to the Philippines from Australia. They sank several Japanese ships. They also liberated 14 high Philippine officers back to Australia.

April 17 '42: Our troops are still fighting the Japanese on the Island of Java under General Schilling. British forces had to withdraw further west in Burma. In the Philippines the Japanese have full control of the main island of Luzon but the Americans are still in control of the small island Corregidor in Manila Bay.

April 18 '42: American planes bombed Yokohama and Tokyo. This is the first time that the Japanese mainland is attacked from the air. The British RAF bombed France with a record 1500 planes. This is a record, The German Air Force record over Britain was 1000.

April 19 '42: Soccer in England. "Free Holland" against "Free France" 2-0. Gen. Marshall, American chief of staff conferred with the British Government and Winston Churchill. He stated that very soon American troops will fully participate in the war and will also go into the European mainland when the time comes. Roman Catholic and Protestant churches proclaimed that they are against Dutch young men going into the German "labor service".

April 20 '42: In Burma, British and Chinese troops have made some advancement. The Germans claim that their U boats have sunk 12 large merchant ships with a tonnage of over 100,000.

April 21 '42: In the Philippines there is continued fighting on the islands of Panay and Cebu. Corregidor is still in American hands and fighting continues. Today is my mother's 47th birthday.

The British landed on the French coast near Boulogne and inflicted considerable damage to German installations. The German press hardly mentioned the operation and called it a 'failed' landing.

April 22 '42: The Germans are building enormous fortifications along the total European coast line. In Holland no person can go on the beach any more. Dutch and Australian forces still fight on the island of Timor in Indonesia.

April 23 '42: I am taking my finals exams for high school: Today; Algebra, Dutch, Trigonometry and Analytical Math. In the USA a factory is being built of 1 by ½ km. In the next year one "Flying fortress" per hour will be built in this huge facility.

April 24 '42: Further final exams for high school: Today; French, German, English and more Math. In

Russia several Polish Divisions under General Anders are ready for the spring offensive against the Germans.

April 25 '42: The German harbor city of Rostock is being heavily bombarded by the British RAF.

April 26 '42: The RAF again bombed Rostock and also the Skoda-factory near Pilsan (Czecho-Slovakia) and the harbor of Cherbourg (France). American troops took possession of the French Islands New Caledonia in the Pacific.

The French General Giraud has escaped German captivity in Dresden (Eastern Germany). The Germans are offering 100,000 marks for his capture. Polish troops are now also stationed in Libya, under the Duke of Gloster, brother of the British King.

April 27 '42: Hitler gave a big speech in which he did not promise a final victory in 1942. He thanked all warriors including those from other countries, who are fighting with the German Army.

April 28'42: Cologne and Drontheim are bombed very heavily by the Allied Air forces. Also St. Thomaire in North France. The escaped French General Giraud was able to make it to Switzerland.

April 29 '42: In Burma the Japanese Air Force is stronger than the Allied Air Force. The Japanese are threatening to take the city of Lashio in Burma. The

Chinese are fighting hard and are blowing the roads up that lead to the City.

April 30 '42: The RAF bombed Drontheim and Kiel, where both German battleships Terpita and Admiral Scheer were located. President Roosevelt gave a radio address. He stated that hundreds of thousands of soldiers are being sent to many fronts. He reassured China that it would be liberated. He also stated that "Flying Fortresses" would play a big role.

May 1 '42: The RAF attacked planes factories around Paris. In the U.S. more than 2 merchant ships a day are being launched.

May 3 '42: Hitler and Mussolini met in Austria with their staffs to discuss further war strategies.

May 4 '42: The Germans bombed Exeter in England and the RAF bombed Hamburg. The German command found 79 Dutch people guilty of sabotage and condemned all of them to death. 72 people were already executed; the others got life imprisonment.

May 5 '42: The French island Madagascar has been occupied by the British marines and the British Army.

May 6 '42: Corregidor (the island in Manila Bay) is now finally in Japanese hands but fighting continues on several of the Philippines islands. In Russia the Germans have to cope with a heavy guerrilla war-force behind their frontlines. The British cruiser Edinburg which escorted convoys to Murmansk (Russia's most Northern harbor) was severely damaged and was sunk by its own command. 90% of the convoy was able to reach Russia.

May 8 '42: The Japanese moving north from Burma crossed the Chinese border. There was a big sea battle between New Guinea and the Solomon Islands, North of Australia. The Japanese lost an aircraft carrier, 2 cruisers and two torpedo boats with heavy damage to others ships.

May 9 '42: The Island of Malta is now under a new commander: Lord Gort, supreme commander of all British Forces in France in 1940.

May 10 '42: The Chinese report success in Burma and Southern China. They are already fighting in the suburbs of Mandalay.

May 11 '42: Guerrilla forces in Serbia are joining with similar troops from Albania and Bulgaria.

May 12 '42: Japan lost a total of 1 ½ million tonnage of merchant ships since the war started. In Indonesia several hundred Dutch people were arrested by the Japanese. In the Netherlands another 24 underground fighters were found guilty of sabotage and were executed by the Germans. The American government has discussions with the French Governor of the Island of Martinique.

May 14 '42: Very hard battles are being fought over the city of Kertsj; on the Crimean peninsula in the Black Sea between German and Russian forces.

May 15 '42: All Dutch military officers were commanded by the Germans to report in 5 cities: Assen, Ede, Breda (my home town), Roermond and Bussum. They were marched to the local railway station and are being transported to Germany as prisoners. The Dutch people are stunned and furious.

May 17 '42: Sir Stafford Cripps stated, on behold of the British Government, that the U.S. and Britain will form a strong second front against Germany on the European continent.

May 18 '42: The largest (so far) contingent of American troops has landed and is disembarking in Northern Ireland, which has become the largest American contingent in Europe.

May 19 '42: General Doolittle, commander of the American Air Force's attack on Japan, reports that a battleship and a cruiser were severely damaged by the American bombs.

May 20 '42: The Dutch Queen, who is in England, appointed Dr. Kasteel as Governor General of the Dutch island of Curacao in the Netherlands Antilles (North of Venezuela).

May 21 '42: Sir Stafford Cripps declared yesterday that England will at the appropriate moment attack Europe's mainland. In Libya both parties are reinforcing themselves.

May 22 '42: The Italian high command reports sinking an American battleship. This is unconfirmed.

May 23 '42:. The congress in Mexico is considering declaring war on Germany and Italy, especially since a large Mexican merchant ship was sunk by a German U boat.

May 23 '42: All non Japanese 17 years and older living in Japanese occupied territories must declare loyalty to Japan. This will include all Dutch people in Indonesia.

May 27 '42: Today I have my oral exams for my high school diploma: Greek, Dutch, Algebra and Trigonometry and Latin.

May 28 '42: Further oral tests for my high school diploma; Today: Physics, Analytical Trigonometry, Chemistry and biology. Apparently I passed! I am lighting my first cigarette on the school grounds. I made a deal with my parents that I would not smoke until age 18 and after graduating from high school. In turn my father gives me 100 guilders.

May 29 '42: Mexico declares war on the "Axis" nations. Large tank battle in Libya.

May 30 '42: Mr Heydrich, chief of the Gestapo and Commissar over Tsjecho-Slovakia has been severely wounded by an attack of a hand grenade.

May 31 '42: Last night more than 100- Allied bombers carried out the largest bombardment of the war. The main target was Cologne. The Allies lost 44 planes. The battle of Cherkoff (Russia) came to an end with no clear winner. Total losses on both sides: 100,000 killed, wounded or captured.

June 1 '42: Final reports of the Cologne bombardment. The damage is indescribable. In total 1250 bombers took part and only 4% of these were shot down. In Libya the Germans made some progress but the British are fighting back hard, especially with their "25 pounder" canons.

June 2 '42: Again over 1000 bombers attacked the Ruhr district. In Libya Rommel's forces were prevented by the British to take the city of Tobruk (close to the Egyptian border). About a total of 100 Tsjech people have been executed by the Germans as a revenge of the attack on Mr. Heydrich.

June 3 '42: Another 21 Tsjech people were executed as revenge on the attack on Heydrich. A multimillion dollar reward for revealing the attacker has not been claimed by anyone.

June 5 '42: Mr. Heydrich died. He is the first prominent German commander to die at the hands of the occupied people. Dutch Harbor (close to Alaska) was attacked by Japanese planes. In Libya British and "Free French" troops are battling General Rommel's attacks.

June 6 '42: Marshall Timoshenko in Russia has so far prevented the Germans to carry out their "spring offensive".

June 7 '42: A Japanese float attacked Midway Island. They lost 2 aircraft carriers, 2 battleships. Two battleships and one aircraft carrier were severely damaged.

June 8 '42: The Russian city of Sebastopol in the Crimea peninsula has been heavily bombed by the Luftwaffe.

June 9 '42: There is heavy fighting in Northern and Western China. General Tsang Kai Chek has a hard time holding his ground.

June 10 '42: America builds weapons at a feverish pace. In Detroit a factory has been completed of one km. length! It produces a "flying fortress" every one hour! In China British and American planes are arriving in great numbers.

June 11 '42: The Germans are still punishing the Czechs for Heydrich's death: A small town has been totally destroyed. All men were executed and women and children taken to concentration camps.

June 12 '42: England and Russia formed an important pact today; signed by Mr. Eden and Mr. Molotoff. The 2 countries plan to solidify a peace in Europe.

June 13 '42: A very large American and large Canadian troop contingent has arrived with tanks etc. in Northern Ireland. In Libya fighting continues. The "Free French" forces under General Odique are making a great contribution to the cause.

June 15 '42: The Japanese Navy has again been hit hard by the American Air Force. Near the Aleutian Islands (off Alaska) one cruiser sunk; 3 cruisers, one aircraft carrier and one destroyer damaged.

June 16 '42: Near Sebastopol, localized fighting took place according to the German news. The German offensive in the area seems to be a little bit diminishing and the Russians recently reinforced the city again. The Russian Black Sea Navy also plays a big part in the defense of the city. In Libya the British troops were split in two by the German forces and they had to withdraw somewhat. The situation for the British is somewhat critical.

June 17 '42: During the last night the RAF again has bombed the Rhine land and the Ruhr territory in Germany.

June 18 '42: In Libya things are not going well for the British; according to a communiqué from Cairo. They had to withdraw from El Adem and other places back to the Egyptian border and are only able to hold Tobruk in Libya. In Russia there is heavy fighting in the Cherkoff front and also near Sebastopol.

June 19 '42: Today two important persons arrived from England in America; firstly Mr. Winston Churchill arrived in the United States for the purpose of important negotiations with Roosevelt.

Secondly our Majesty Queen Wilhelmina of the Netherlands has arrived in the United States in a special plane provided by the president. The purpose of her visit amongst other things is to visit her daughter and grandchildren whom she has not seen for about two years. The Germans report today that the northern half of Sebastopol has been occupied by them.

June 20 '42: Near Sebastopol the situation is basically unchanged; in Libya the situation is serious. The Germans have penetrated the outskirts of Tobruk and it doesn't look good for the British trying to defend the city.

June 21 '42: Tobruk has fallen to the Germans. Apparently Tobruk is not totally in German hands. The British had to withdraw westward over the Egyptian border. In the Far East not very much is changing but the Japanese threat towards Australia remains according to Australian Prime Minister Curtin.

June 22 '42: Tobruk is now completely in German hands and also the enforced town of Bardia had to be cleared by the British. The British of course had to withdraw further east over of the Egyptian border. The pressure on Sebastopol is still very serious but the defenders don't give up and try to defend each inch of ground. The Germans had put in five divisions and even the Rumanians are helping the Germans with two divisions.

June 23 '42: The RAF has bombed Emden in Germany very heavily. The attack was carried out by a strong force. Emden is one of the most important U boat bases of the Germans and it should be kept in mind that the submarines are one of the greatest dangers for the Allied troops; because they have sank a lot of tonnage in the last couple of years. The ships are very important for the transport of war material from the factories to the front. In this particular case, from America to Russia, England, the Far East and the Mediterranean.

June 24 '42: The Germans made further advances near Cherkoff.

June 25 '42: The Germans made some advances in Egypt. The British absolutely had to abandon Solloem, Fort Capuzzo and Sidi El Berrani and completely withdraw further towards Alexandria in Egypt.

June 26 '42: The RAF carried out one of the largest bombardments in the history of the war. At least 1,000 planes bombed in particular Bremen in Germany and also Cologne and Essen. An enormous amount of damage was inflicted and the RAF lost about 52 planes.

June 27 '42: British Prime Minister Winston Churchill has returned from his third visit to America since the beginning of the war. He met with President Roosevelt and had long negotiations. Both Washington and London stated that the operations which are being carried out by the Allies will break the power of the German Military, particularly on the Russian front. They also stated that they will support especially Russia and China. Roosevelt stated that America built 4000 planes in the month of May. That is an enormous number of planes. Compare that to Germany's building about 2000 planes per month. Italy about 500 per month and Japan about 1000 per month; England about 2000 per month.

June 28 '42: There is a heavy battle between the Germans and the British going on which probably will decide what will happen to the Suez Canal. In Russia the situation is mostly unchanged on the front. It is stated that Hitler is now finally starting his spring offensive.

June 29 '42: The Germans report to have taken the city of Mersah Matrou in Egypt. That has not been confirmed by the British.

June 30 '42: Mersah Matrou is now definitely in German hands and on the east of the city a big battle is taking place. General Auchinleck who is the British Superior Commander in the near East has taken command of the British troops in Egypt. Last night Bremen has been bombed again very heavily by the RAF.

July 1 '42: The Germans are making progress in Egypt, going east. Apparently they are only about 100 miles away from Alexandria. There is heavy fighting taking place near Kursk and Sebastopol in Russia. The last city is being attacked by heavy German artillery and planes. The city is absolutely in ruins; however the defenders have not given up.

July 2 '42: The British parliament rejected a motion of 475 against 25 to criticize the government. Which means that the British people in spite of the setbacks in Libya and Egypt support the government. Churchill again gave a speech where he expressed personally that things didn't go too well in the Middle East but that the British finally will defeat the Germans. Sebastopol is now completely in German hands. Even though still some fighting in the city is still taking place.

July 3 '42: The British are still holding El Alamein which is about 65 kilometers west of Alexandria and have beaten back the German attacks. In Russia the Germans are now moving forward on a broad front. Bremen has again been bombed very heavily by the RAF through the night.

July 4 '42: Headline; the first American planes are now over Europe. Last night 12 planes coming from British airfields bombed three cities in the Netherlands. Six of these planes were Americans. These are the first American planes who appeared from Britain over Europe.

July 5 '42: The Germans broke through the Russian front at a few sites. The Russians are working very hard to move the war industry eastward to the Ural Mountains. A new city has been created called Aviagrad. This city will only produce planes.

July 6 '42: Because of the happenings of the last two days the situation in Egypt has changed. The British established themselves strongly in the positions near El Alamein, while the Germans, who try to break through the British fortifications, are not be able to do so.

July 7 '42: Today is the fifth birthday of the war between China and Japan. The Chinese lost six million people against the Japanese two million in that period of time. This very large difference is due to their weapons. Chinese weapons were getting much better because of the British and American deliveries. Today also the news came that the American bombers starting from a base in China caused severe damage in Japan. They were able to destroy 65 planes on the ground. They themselves only lost 12 planes.

July 8 '42: In Egypt the heavy fighting continues. And in the South the British were able to move ahead somewhat. The Germans had to withdraw but the British stayed close on the German tail. In 1941 Britain has sent 10,000 planes and 3,000 tanks overseas. That is an amazing number.

July 13 '42: I was with my brother on a sailboat. We collapsed and went into the water. It is interesting that it is taking place on the 13th. In the Netherlands 13 is supposed to be a bad number.

July 17 '42: We are in Loosdrecht which is a small town on a lake in the Netherlands; we are happy to be on vacation. In one week we have not been able to see people or been able to listen to the radio. That is why I could not report my daily reports. However today I heard that in Egypt heavy fighting is still taking place near El Alamein. El Alamein is still in British hands.

July 18 '42: The Russians are retreating under heavy German bombardment. And in a few places they had to withdraw over the Don River although they were able to hold the city of Woronez. The Germans are trying to reach the Caucasian Mountains in spite of heavy Russian defense.

July 19 '42: In the meantime, in the diplomatic world some things are happening between the United States and Vichy; Vichy is of course the portion of southern France which had not been occupied by the German Army. Vichy has a neutral government. The

164

Americans tried to have some access to the French fleet which still consists of a battleship, four cruisers, a few torpedo boats and a submarine. The Americans are trying to persuade Vichy to have these ships travel to an American Harbor and then be used on the Allied side. So far Vichy has denied the request of the Americans.

July 20'42: In Egypt the situation has been completely consolidated. However there is more initiative on the side of the British.

July 21 '42: Strong rumors are going around about a possible landing in France, in particular in the occupied countries, also Norway has been named. These are loose rumors and a lot of these are based on wishful thinking of course. At home suddenly today the Germans are confiscating bicycles and have installed a lot of a barbed wire near the coast.

July 22 '42: The Germans have now proclaimed that all Dutch people who do not have absolute need for bicycles must hand them over to the authorities. In Russia near Voronezh, the Russian Army has been able to stop the Germans and pushed them back somewhat. However in the South the Germans have made some progress. In particular the city of Worosjilofgrad apparently has been occupied by the Germans. In Egypt the situation is basically unchanged.

July 23 '42: There is still talk about a possible invasion of mainland Europe by the British but there is more talk than reality.

July 24 '42: Thousands of Dutch people have been taken as hostages by the Germans. This is a very serious situation. (I had a list of the people who were taken as hostages in Noord-Brabant which is the province in which I live. However unfortunately I somehow lost this list. I had no notes for the next few days.)

July 31 '42: We returned home from our vacation near the lake at Loosdrecht, where we did a lot of sailing on the lake. Things are not going too well for the Russians. Rostof has been occupied by the Germans. They also made great progress east of the city. Near Voronezh still heavy fighting is going on. In Russia one of the most serious situations is the situation of the Caucasus which of course is the huge mountain range north to south which divides Russia and Siberia. The large oil fields are located there. If the Caucasus falls totally in German hands that would be a very serious situation. In Egypt in the Far East the situation is basically unchanged. The RAF again bombed the city of Hamburg heavily.

August 1 '42: The Russians had pulled back somewhat in the South. Last night the city of Dusseldorf has been bombed heavily by 30 planes of the RAF.

August 6 '42: In the last few days I stayed with a farmer in Beek and I was not able to listen to the radio and make notes. Two situations are very important. In the first place, on the Russian front the Germans have been able to penetrate somewhat. On the Russian front the Germans advanced somewhat deeper into the Caucasus Mountains. This is probably not a very good thing but on the other hand we can report that is absolutely the only sector were the Germans operated aggressively and make progress and contrast by a year ago on the beginning of the Russian campaign when the German Army progressed also in the North and in the South and at that time the Germans got into Leningrad and got close to Moscow. In some ways we notice a decrease in the German offensive. It is interesting also that in general in the occupied countries more and more one expects a second front which means a British and American landing in Europe. This feeling also is carried by the occupiers because left and right they pick up prisoners. Also the order to turn in bicycles is a sign that the Germans become more nervous about a possible second front. There is also a rumor that the island of Walcheren on the far west coast of the Netherlands may be totally evacuated by the Germans, and the population will be transported eastwards to the province of Brabant and will be stationed there.

August 9 '42: As mentioned before we notice the tension amongst the Germans and that's continuing.

August 10 '42: The strategic situation in Russia is about the same. Two more cities were occupied by the Germans. Another important happening is the American landing on the Solomon's Islands north of Australia which were occupied in the beginning of the Japanese-American war. Apparently strong Allied fleets are present in the area. It is also interesting that in India the very famous leader Gandhi has been arrested together with other prominent people.

August 12 '42: The British aircraft carrier Eagle has been sunk by German U boats. The ship had 22, 000 tons and was built in 1910.

The Germans have penetrated further into the Caucasus Mountains and also furthered their offensive in the direction of Stalingrad which is of course strongly in Russian hands. I myself am staying with my uncle Oom Max. Everybody has to be home by 10:00 O'clock because of the German order and because an attack which was made on a German radio station in the Netherlands.

August 13 '42: Mainz has been bombed in Germany by the RAF two nights in a row. The British-American air offensive is strong and persistent.

August 14 '42: In the Mediterranean Sea a British convoy was attacked by German U Boats. Britain has reported that recently of course the Eagle was lost but they also lost the 9,000 ton cruiser Manchester. However they sank two German U boats.

168

August 15 '42: The five first hostages whom the Germans arrested Sunday August the 9th in connection with the bombing which took place in Rotterdam had been executed today.

August 16 '42: The Germans advanced somewhat in the direction of Stalingrad and the city is gradually in greater danger.

August 17 '42: Winston Churchill went to Moscow and had conferences with Stalin. General Wavell the British General in the Middle East was also present at the meeting. Churchill returned to London today.

August 18 '42: The city of Osnabruck was bombarded heavily by the British Air Force. General Alexander is replacing General Auchinleck as British Commander in the Middle East. General Montgomery is replacing General Richie as Commander of the 8th British Army which is stationed mostly in Egypt.

August 19 '42: There was a British landing in France. The British landed on the French coast. The British tanks were able to fight the Germans because of good air cover. The attack was carried out by British, Canadian and French troops and took place near Dieppe in France. They were able to destroy many German fortifications and then withdraw back to Britain. Britain made this very clear; this is not an invasion, just a raid.

August 20 '42: Two nights ago the British bombed West Germany and the Russian parts of Prussia and also Danzig and Konigsbergen. There is some tension between Brazil and Germany. More and more Brazilian ships have been torpedoed by German U Boats. As a result people have been protesting in Brazil. The Brazilian planes have been able to sink 5 German U Boats in the southern part of the Atlantic Ocean.

August 21 '42: The Russians bombarded Germany for the second time in particular parts of Prussia and Silesia. In the meantime the Germans were able to penetrate into Caucasus a little bit more; the situation for Stalingrad is not good. About a year ago the Germans started the occupation of Leningrad; after one year the situation has not changed. There is a standoff because the Red Army has been able to hold the Germans back.

August 22 '42: The two South American countries Brazil and Uruguay today declared war against Germany.

August 23 '42: The RAF today bombed Emden and were able to destroy important parts of the Harbor.

August 24 '42: New American troops arrived with their tanks in Britain. Interestingly in Brazil a secret German airfield was detected about 1,000 kilometers from the capitol of Brazil.

August 26 '42: The Germans moved a little further in the direction of Stalingrad. In the area of Moscow, a counter offensive was starting and the Russians were able to move the Germans back about 25 to 30 miles.

August 27, 42: The Solomon Islands are now completely in American hands. The Japanese tried to re-conquer the Islands but they did not succeed. The Duke of Kent in Britain, the youngest son of King George V of England, was trying to move to Iceland but apparently his plane crashed over Scotland and he was killed.

August 28 '42: The Dutch Queen came back from America to Britain. The RAF bombed Nuremberg. About 30 British planes did not return home.

August 29 '42: The Germans are not able to move further around Stalingrad. The Germans also met strong Russian resistance in the Caucasus and are not able to move further there either. Near Moscow the German Army has been pushed back by the Russians.

August 30 '42: Berlin was bombed heavily by four engine Russian bombers. About 46 fires were started by them. The Chinese have been able to conquer two airfields, which they took back from the Japanese. This is also important because from the airfields, Tokyo can be attacked by air.

August 31 '42: Today is the Queen's birthday. The Queen's birthday in England was enthusiastically celebrated mostly in the one part of the Dutch empire which was not occupied by the enemy.

This part is "the West Indies", which means the Dutch colonies in South America in particular the Island of Curacao.

September 4 '42: The battle in Egypt is in full swing. The site of the battle is about 25 miles south of El Alamein. Near Stalingrad the Russians had to withdraw somewhat and also in the Caucasus Mountains they had to lose some territory.

September 13 '42: I was not able to record for a couple of weeks because I was in Amsterdam following a course of medical analyst. I share a room with my buddy Fons Walder. (It is interesting that my friend, Fons, later on studied at the University of Nijmegen and became a professor in Neurosurgery and after that he became finally president of the International Organization for Neurosurgeons.) Also this week I had visited my aunt Lies and my uncle Muk.

September 16 '42: Her Royal Highness Princess Juliana of the Netherlands in Canada announced that she is expecting a baby in January.

September 19 '42: In the last few days there is not much news from the front. The threats for Stalingrad are getting larger. The Germans said that they penetrated in the south of the city. The Far East is basically unchanged. Germany has been bombed by the British and American air forces.

September 22 '42: Last night I returned from Amsterdam back home and I am going to review the military situation around the world. In Russia in general not much has changed; enormous fighting is taking place in Stalingrad with very large numbers of casualties, but this large city on the Wolga River is still holding up. There is also continuous fighting in the Caucasus Mountains although the most fighting in the Caucasus takes place near Mosdok. In Egypt there are no major changes. In the Far East the center of the battle is still in the Solomon Islands.

Saturday September 26 '42: The British occupied the capital of Tananarivo on the Island of Madagascar.

September 27 '42: Heavy fighting still continues around Stalingrad. Also in the Caucasus Mountains heavy battles are taking place. After a weekend at home I am returning tomorrow to Amsterdam.

October 8 '42: In Stalingrad heavy fighting continues. The Germans are still not able the completely occupy the city.

October 11 '42: In Stalingrad fighting continues. The Germans are saying that a strategic purpose has been reached.

October 16 '42: Unfortunately we have to report that more hostages have been taken and have to give their lives for our country. As punishment for sabotage activities from our underground fighters

15 Dutch hostages have been executed by the Germans.

October 17 '42: The battle in Stalingrad is very heavy. Apparently the Germans have been able to make some progress into the city thanks to their Air Force and artillery. In other news American troops arrived in Liberia in West Africa. On the African west coast the Allied Forces have six sites of military fortifications. Gambia, Sierra Leone, Liberia, the Gold Coast, Nigeria and French Equatorial Africa.

October 18 '42: The Germans have not been able to make any further progress in Stalingrad. In the defense of Malta which of course is a British island in the Mediterranean Sea, they have been attacked by the German Air Force very heavily but were able to defend the territory and brought down about 114 enemy planes. The British Air Force has bombed the factory which manufactures war material in France.

October 19 '42: The Russians reported today that they have to withdraw of a small section of Stalingrad.

October 21 '42: The British Admiralty reported in England that on the memorial day of the battle near Trafalgar, 2 battle ships have been launched of the King George V Class, the very famous 35,000 ton ships.

October 24 '42: In Egypt again major battles are taking place, the British starting a big offensive;

further details are expected soon.

October 25 '42: The British offensive in Egypt is making some progress. An Italian and German convoy in the Mediterranean was attacked and 17 ships sank. One cruiser and torpedo boat were part of the ships that were sunk. In Stalingrad the Russians had launched a new attack and were able to recapture a small portion of the city. Last night the British bombed Milan in Italy heavily, some major factories are located in Milan.

October 31 '42: The situation is Stalingrad is stationary.

November 2 '42: Progress is being reported by the British in respect to their offensive in Egypt. The Australians have been able to make some progress in New Guinea.

November 3 '42: The situation in Stalingrad has changed somewhat in favor of the Russians. In the Caucasus Mountains the Germans have not been able to make any significant progress. Kokoda and New Guinea has been recaptured by the Australians from the Japanese. A large tank battle is taking place in Egypt.

November 4 '42: The British 8th Army has made some progress in Egypt. The situation in Stalingrad is unchanged.

November 5 '42: Rommel, who is the main General in charge of the German Forces in Egypt is in full retreat westward because of the pressure of the 8th British Army. General Rommel may have lost about half of his planes and half of his tanks. A German General has been captured and 9,000 prisoners were taken by the British.

November 6 '42: The British Army in Egypt has made 120 kilometers progress and had passed the city of Foeka by 20 kilometers; they captured 13,000 German forces. The French in Madagascar are asking for the cessation of activities. Stalin gave a big speech at the location of the 25th anniversary of the Russian Revolution.

November 7 '42: Today is the 100th day of the battle of Stalingrad. In total the British have captured 20,000 prisoners in Egypt. The RAF has bombed the city of Genoa last night. The Luftwaffe which is the German Air Force is almost unnoticed now over Egypt. The RAF is now more and more the master of the skies.

November 8 '42: Big news aired today. A second front has been started. American troops from England landed in French Northwest Africa in cooperation with the British Forces from Gibraltar. The first landings went well. The landings took place near Algiers and other locations of the Atlantic Coast. The Supreme Commander of this operation is General Eisenhower and the Naval Forces are under Admiral Cunningham. Marshall Petain who is in charge of the Southern portion of France, which is not occupied by the German Forces, made a statement from Vichy

176

which is the capital of that area that the French will defend their territory.

November 9 '42: Algiers has surrendered to the American troops. Two airfields were occupied by the American Forces. French resistance against these activities of the American forces is minimum.
The remaining German forces under General Rommel have retreated over the Egyptian-Libyan border going westward. Admiral Darlan from France is in Algiers. He is either a prisoner or he may have gone over to the American side.

November 10 '42: The Americans are making progress in Morocco and had occupied Oran. In the harbor of Casablanca the French battle ship Jean Bart was occupied. Six large transports have arrived in Algiers. British troops are battling the remaining German troops and have made further progress. In the last six days General Rommel has withdrawn a further 400 kilometers westward. General Giraud from France is now working with the American troops and tries to organize the French Army for the Allies.

November 11 '42: This morning German troops have entered the unoccupied part of France which was left to the free French up to now. The purpose is to reach the Mediterranean Sea. Petain who is the President of Southern France has protested against this move. The French in Casablanca reported their fleet has gone over to the allied site. Roosevelt stated that the plans to invade North Africa were already put together in July. Churchill gave a big speech in England; he said that important things will happen in the near future.

November 12 '42: In West North Africa there is a battle involving Tunis, which is where the American troops are heading. In Egypt British Forces have make further progress.

November 13 '42: Tobruk and Bardia have been occupied today by the British. General Rommel has probably lost about 80,000 men up to now. Admiral Darlan has now completely chosen the Allied side and is organizing the French fleet in Toulon to join the allied forces. There is still heavy fighting taking place in Stalingrad but not as heavy as previously. The temperature is 15° Celsius below zero. The French General who is the commander of the French Army in Morocco is now completely cooperating with General Eisenhower.

November 14 '42: The American and British have made further progress in Tunisia and have crossed the Tunisian border. Genoa has been bombed again by the British. Near Stalingrad the Russians are noticing that the German Luftwaffe is weaker than previously. Further progress has been made by the British in Egypt. General Darlan, the French General has now been put in charge of the defense of Algiers.

November 15 '42. This morning in England from 9 to 12 am all the clocks are sounding celebrating the progress in Egypt. From June 1940 all clocks were quiet in England with the purpose to use them only in the eventual invasion by the Germans which of course never took place. American troops crossed the border of Tunisia marching towards the capital of Tunisia. The British troops in Egypt are making further progress westward. There are strong signs that the major German and Italian troops in North Africa and Libya have been moved back to Tripoli. The British troops made 25 miles progress today. In Stalingrad the Russians were able to beat back the German attacks. Genoa has been bombed again last night.

November 17 '42: In Libya further progress has been made by the British troops. General Rommel is pulling back his German Army. In the Far East a large sea battle took place near the Solomon Islands, which is labeled the largest success in the history of the American Navy. Many Japanese ships were sunk by the American Forces. One battle ship, 2 heavy and 3 light cruisers, 5 torpedo boats, 8 transport ships and 5 supply ships. On New Guinea the Australian and American forces are making further progress northwards.

November 18 '42: The British troops have moved forward in North Africa to within 17 miles of Benghazi. British and American parachute forces have occupied airfields in Tunisia.

November 19 '42: A large battle is taking place south of Benghazi in Libya.

November 20 '42: Benghazi has been cleared by the German forces, who have apparently withdrawn towards Tripoli. A tank battle took place in Tunis between the American and German troops. 11 German tanks were destroyed. In the Caucasus the Russians were able to destroy a German tank division.

November 21 '42: Benghazi in Libya is now occupied completely by the British troops.

November 22 '42: In Libya further battles are taking place. The Russians were able today to cross the River Don northwest of Stalingrad. The RAF bombed Turin in Italy very heavily.

November 23 '42: The Russians have captured the city of Kalatsj in the Don River area. The German troops which moved ahead in Stalingrad are being threatened to be cut off because of the advancement of some Russian troops coming from the Northwest and the Southwest of Stalingrad. French West Africa including Dakar and the French Navy which is located near that city have now completely joined the Allies. Including in this are some French colonies like Gold Coast, Togo, Dahome etc. The advancement of the American-Australian forces in New Guinea is continuing. The forward movement of the American troops on Guadalcanal on the Solomon Islands is making progress also.

November 25 '42: The British troops in Libya have conquered another small city. The French governor of French West Africa declared in a radio comment that all of French West Africa will be joining the allied troops under the command of Admiral Darlan.

November 26 '42: The Russians are moving forward and have reconquered a good deal of the city. Northwest of Stalingrad they advanced 25 kilometers. Three German divisions have been captured with their generals.

November 27 '42: The Mediterranean main French harbor of Toulon where the French fleet was stationed has been occupied by the Germans. The fleet consists of battle ships and some cruisers, also 25 torpedo boats and 20 U boats. However the Germans were not able to capture these since the French had already sunk these ships. In Tunisia the British have made further progress.

November 29 '42: The first British Army in Tunisia has been able to move within 50 miles west of Tunis. The Russian Army near Stalingrad has been able to capture some more territory. West of Moscow the Russians started an offensive and have inflicted heavy losses against the Germans. Last night the RAF has bombed Turin in Italy and inflicted heavy damage.

November 30 '42: The connections between Biserta and Tunis have been broken by the British and American troops. They are marching closer and closer towards the capital of Tunisia.

December 1 '42: The Germans are more and more cut off near the city of Stalingrad and there is a greater chance that the Germans will be completely cut off. Near Tunis the British and American forces broke through the first German army units, and reached Tunis to within 12 miles. The French Island of Reunion near Madagascar which is off the east coast of Africa has been captured by the British forces. 3 French U Boats arrived in Algiers.

December 2 '42: The number of Germans killed near Stalingrad is estimated at the moment of 64,000 people. Admiral Darlan of the French Forces is declared as the head of the New liberated France with Algeria as capital.

December 3 '42: The German convoy on its way to Tunis has been attacked by the British fleet and air force. 4 transport ships and 2 torpedo boats were sunk by the British Air Force. It has been reported that by the American landing in North Africa last month, the Dutch torpedo boat Isaac Sweers was lost.

December 6 '42: Today the RAF has bombed the city of Eindhoven which is only some 50 miles from my home town. The famous Philips factories which are famous for its electronics has been totally destroyed. Some of the British planes flew over our home city of Breda.

December 7 '42: It is one year ago when the Japanese Air Force attacked Pearl Harbor. Many American planes were lost at that time; however the battle ship Arizona which was destroyed has been renovated and is now in action.

December 14 '42: The 8th British Army near El Alamein in Libya has broken through German forces and apparently the Germans are about to retreat under General Rommel going west. They will probably try to connect with the German forces in Tunis.

ADDEMDUM II
MY DIARY OF THE LAST TWO MONTHS LEADING UP TO OUR LIBERATION BY THE ALLIED FORCES: SEPTEMBER AND OCTOBER 1944.

We were somewhat worn out by the stresses of the war, listening to the radio to receive, hopefully, good news and to look again and again at the map to see if, and how much, progress was made in the last few days. The exciting thing now is that we no longer look at the map of North Africa or the Pacific. We are actually looking at distances within 300 to 500 miles from our home town!

September 2 '44: My father went fishing and we are helping my mother with household chores. Our friend Kees Vogel comes to visit us and says, "you should listen to the radio: There is good news. British troops have crossed Belgium's Southern border and occupied Tournai." After lunch we hear even more exciting news. Brussels, Belgium's capital, has fallen to the British. Imagine how they are celebrating there! This is the fourth European capital taken by the Allies! First Rome, (June 5th), Paris (August 22), Bucharest (taken by the Russians) and now Brussels.

September 3 '44: I am meeting with my close friends Maarthen and Henk Hofman (we are calling ourselves the "Triumvirate" the three man bond) and our lady friends. (Henk would only live about 8 weeks after that. He was executed by a German firing squad). We are excitedly watching a long column of German troops returning eastward.

September 4 '44: Pappie, who is a dentist, has gone to treat his patients at his office downtown. However very exciting news is coming through: Antwerp has been occupied by British troops, which is only about 50 miles from Breda! The retreat eastward of the German troops is visibly increasing; we can see it from our front window across the lake and many people are standing on the streets watching. (We had no idea that our liberation would still be about 7 weeks later) Somehow it is a sad sight to see the proud German soldiers lying asleep in trucks and cars, looking dreary and worn out. Here and there you see soldiers with their Parisian girlfriends, who remained loyal to their man. Pappie has been able to take photos and movies of this scenery.

September 5 '44: We keep watching the German retreat, but we sort of resent that the retreat is rather orderly and the British should be here by now and take care of these Germans. To mess up the orderly retreat we remove and hide some of the direction signs from the street and around the lake, which results in some of the Germans going in the wrong direction. Ironically we hear on the radio news from America that Breda has fallen to the British. We know that is untrue. The newspaper on September 4 publishes an announcement from the SS High commander in Holland that people have to stay indoors certain hours of the day and that suspicious gatherings of Dutch citizens will be shot at.

September 6 '44: The Germans appear to move more Southward rather than Eastward. The news tells us that the British march Northwards from France, resulting in the conquest of Brussels and Antwerp and then the crossing of the Albert canal. This may have been a little too fast. The Germans were able to cut some of the British troops off. This would explain the more general Southward movement of the German troops.

Our liberation now again seems somewhat further away. Apparently on the Dutch Island of Curacao in the West Indies Breda's "liberation" was prematurely celebrated.

The pressure of the occupation is now again increasing. Bicycles are taken by the Germans across town and boys and men are being taken to work for the German Army. Five Breda citizens were arrested by the Germans and executed. Two of them were Dr. Scheffelaar and the artist Feitze de Bruyn. At home, Rob, my brother and I, are now fully occupied with housework (my older sister, Liesje, now 22 years old, works further North in Utrecht as a nurse in a hospital. We have no contact with her; my younger sister, Anne Marie is 10 years old). Cooking is more difficult now.

Gas has now been restricted from 7-8:30 a.m., 11-2 p.m. and from 5-8 p.m. We now eat more from our stored food since we expect to be liberated in the not too distant future.

September 7 '44: A large German truck stops in front of our house. May be they are confiscating bicycles. We quietly move our 2 best cycles to the back of our property and leave my mother's cycle in the front. Our small radio is carefully hidden. Our front door bell rings loudly. My brother Rob, his friend Kees and myself also quickly move to the backyard. The German police comes in, rejects our bicycle and leaves. We were lucky. In the evening Pappie and Mammie go to a farm and return to our joy with a large supply of potatoes.

There is not much news from the front. The allies apparently are regrouping to get ready for a new offensive. The front line now apparently runs from West to East roughly in Northern Belgium and further West goes southward towards Luxemburg and Nancy.

September 8 '44: Things in Breda are again getting a little more normal! The baker and the butcher are again calling on our house, most shops are again open and many people are going to work. However most men are not going outside, because many have been taken by the Germans to work for the military. The small military progress in our neighborhood is frustrating but elsewhere great progress takes place: the British made great progress in Italy, the Russians move into Yugo-Slavia from Rumania, further progress in France etc.

September 9 '44: The German appointed mayor announces that no further men will be arrested by the Germans to work for the military, provided that those, who were already taken, will continue to work for the Germans. Apparently Queen Wilhelmina in her British home was hit by a flying bomb, but she was not hurt. The news tells us that the British have started a new offensive in France and Belgium towards Germany. Princess Juliana has moved back from Ottawa to London hoping to return to a liberated Holland soon. The Dutch brigade "Princess Irene", part of the British Army, apparently is ready to move towards their home country under the command of prince Bernhard (Juliana's husband).

Gas has been rationed further, so cooking becomes more difficult. Fortunately we have some oil. In the morning we share cups of our last real tea and biscuits.

Apparently some Dutch people were in a hurry and celebrated their liberation already, even going as far as standing on the roads with flowers to welcome the allied liberators.

A good sign of the allied progress is the presence of British and American planes in our skies, attacking the German military. General Eisenhower announced that some Dutch territory had been liberated. This was incorrect and later on that news was cancelled.

September 11 '44: We are working hard doing household chores. Pappie went to his dental office at the usual hour but came home at 11 a.m. We wondered why he came home so early. He said that he had received information that many bridges would be closed and that the whole city was about to be closed off. Pappie decided that for the time being he would not go to his dental practice.

The latest news tells us that Belgium Zeebrugge and Blankenberge have been liberated and lo and behold the small town of Cadzand in the Netherlands on the North Sea has been liberated: the first piece of real estate of Holland is free! (It is exciting that several years ago we went to Cadzand on our summer vacation with the family). Also just South of Eindhoven, about 40 miles East of us (where the famous Philips Electronics factories are located even today) British troops are only a few miles from the Dutch border. The allied forces are only 15 km. from the German City of Achen. American fighter planes are very active over our part of the world. My girlfriend Jetje will come tomorrow for a visit to help with polishing our brass and copper and will stay for dinner.

September 12 '44: The weather is beautiful. We had several friends over, including Jetje. We studied the maps and the Allied progress and all of us helped polish our brass. Then we had a nice walk around the lake. The activity in the air from the Allied planes is increasing so Anne Marie, my younger sister, who is 9 years old, is not going to school.

The official news is now confirmed and Allied troops are now on Dutch territory. Eupen and Luxemburg were occupied by the Allies and they are now 10 km North of Trier in Germany. Local news tells us that again local men have been taken by the Germans to work for the military. Rumors have it that the Germans are planning to blow up large and important buildings in our city.

September 14 '44: We cleaned windows at home today and applied strips of paper in case of breakage by bombs etc. We are considering applying outside boards which means that we will have no daylight for some time. Schools are now closed because of firing from the Allied planes on the city. Generally speaking we are hearing more explosions. We are in luck. Robje was able to pick up 20 jars of jam because the jam factory is cleaning up their extra supplies.

The first German town, called Rötchen, has been taken by the Americans. Today the Germans took some of the men, working for factories, to work for the German military.

September 15 '44: The city of Maastricht in the very Southern part of Holland has been taken by the Americans! In the Far East two important islands in Indonesia have been taken by the Allies. They are now 450 km from the Philippines.

Our town is more and more isolated. There is no more post and the telephone is working poorly. Train traffic has halted. We still see Allied Aircraft regularly but no more German Luftwaffe for some time. Salt is getting scarce.

September 16 '44: We are busy doing house work. Jetje came over for a visit at 4 p.m. The news from Maastricht is of large celebrations and everywhere you see the orange colors (our royal family is from "The House of Orange" a town in Southern France; from where our first prince came in the 1600's) One also saw many young ladies with bald scalps (they were punished by the public because they had fraternized with the Germans).

September 17 '44: The day started normally. It is Sunday. Many people are on the street and are looking at the sky. We are looking at an unforgettable sight. Hundreds of Allied bombers are pulling smaller gliders going eastward. Later on we learn that about 50 to 100 km further East, still over Dutch territory, the gliders get "unhooked", land on fields and load thousands of troops with small tanks, trucks and cars and occupy the land trying to defeat the German military. This is probably the largest landing in military history and must have taken enormous planning. The BBC then informed us about this huge operation, the announcement started with the Dutch National Anthem. For the sake of history this was called "Operation Market Garden". The plan was to liberate all Southern Holland, South of the Rhine River and from there to cross the 2 major rivers which divided Southern Holland from mid and Northern Holland and capture the city of Arnhem.

At home we tried to sew a British flag together. The news is that Hulst, the second Dutch city after Maastricht has fallen and was liberated by Polish troops.

I am hearing explosions in the distance. Are those the British after 4 ½ years of occupation?

September 18 '44: According to the British news the landings were successful with light to moderate losses and several smaller Dutch towns were liberated. Apparently some Dutch commando's were amongst the Allied troops. We have been watching the activity in the air from the roof of one of our neighbors. Thousands larger and smaller planes with gliders were passing us by in the air. What an incredible sight!

Rob and I went in the park around the lake and were able to again remove some smaller road signs to confuse the retreating Germans. Pappie has not been going to work. He plays a lot of bridge and reads a lot. My 10 year old sister Mietsie (Anne Marie) has been very active with friends. Although she is young she asks a lot of questions about the war and follows its progress. She and her friends loudly cheer the Allied planes going overhead.

September 19 '44: Apparently Eindhoven is now fully in British hands. From there they moved northwards and progressed 48 kilometers in 24 hours. They are now to within 8 km. of the city of Nijmegen. We have also heard that the British Army crossed the border north of Antwerp into Dutch territory. Radio Orange from London warns young and middle age men to be careful not to be arrested by the Germans. Another order came from the Queen to the Railway system in order to close out all railway traffic as much as possible.

Pappie and Mammie went to visit Oom Gé to celebrate his birthday and Jetje came to visit me. We are now listening much more to the radio, which we always had to hide for several years. Our British flag which we sewed together is now finished. We are now starting on an American flag.

September 20 '44: There is heavy fighting in the streets of Nijmegen but the British were not yet able to cross the Waal River. There is also fighting near Arnhem. Jetje came to visit and told us that a large number of German troops are moving West and North. They are probably concentrating to cross the Rhine and move into the Northern 2/3 of Holland as a last stand.
Along the West coast on the North Sea the Germans are still in St. Nazaire in Bretagne, Calais, Boulogne and Dunkirk. The Russians are making progress on the Eastern front. They are now in Latvia and Estonia and are close to Riga.

September 21 '44: Important news: British and American forces have successfully crossed the bridge over the Waal River north of Nijmegen and try to move North to Arnhem. However the German SS troops are putting up heavy resistance. Polish troops liberated Terneuzen (Northwest of Antwerp) Mr. Seyss-Inquart, the German high commissioner for Holland has apparently gone back to Germany.

September 22 '44: British troops near Arnhem are involved in heavy battles. They were not able to make much progress. The German resistance is very fierce and powerful. In Italy Allied Greek troops have taken the city of Rimini. The American Army is now halfway between Florence and Bologna. The Russians are making further progress in the Baltic countries. Here in Breda the Dutch police have been disarmed and is being replaced by the S.S.!

September 23 '44: Fighting near Arnhem is fierce. The Allies have not been able to cross the Rhine River. The British landing forces North of the Rhine are having a very hard time against the German S.S. Apparently some Allied troops are halfway between Eindhoven and Tilburg. That is only 30-40 km. east of Breda!

In Italy the Allies are very close to the planes of the Po River north of Florence and the Futa pass was reached and the 8th Army is moving further north. The Russians reached the Gulf of Riga in the Baltics after taking the important harbor at PERNAU. The Russians also made good progress from Rumania and are now about to enter the Hungarian planes. Total German loses in World War II so far are over 3 million.

September 24 '44: The battle near Arnhem goes on relentlessly. The 5th American Army is making great progress in Italy in the direction of Bologna. Finish troops keep fighting the Germans in Finland. In Poland, Russians troops crossed a major river near Warsaw and connected Polish freedom fighters under General Bor-Komorowski.

In our house nobody goes to work or to school any more. We all help with household chores; a very unusual situation. Many people come outside and chat with their friends and neighbors. It is an eery feeling that the British troops are only 30-40 km. from us. There is no more Post or telephone.

A sample of unusual time: yesterday a boy came down with meningitis and was carried by his father on foot all the way to Breda Hospital. It took him 3 1/2 hours. Many wounded German soldiers are being admitted to our local hospitals.

September 26 '44: Several friends come to visit, including Jetje. I am getting a fever in the evening and probably have the flu.

The battle of Arnhem continues in full swing. The situation near Arnhem is not so good for the British. Estonia is completely in Russian hands.

September 27 '44: Not good news: The British North of the Rhine River near Arnhem have surrendered. With deep respect and gratitude we memorialize all young British who gave their lives in this battle. Near

Eindhoven thousands of volunteers helped to rebuild the airport which is now again open and available to the Allies. Belgium now has a new government, which contains 2 communists, which is historically a new feature.

September 28 '44: Churchill gave an important speech. He stated that it is possible that the war will not be over this year but will run into next year. He also stated that there are now 2 to 3 million Allied troops in Western Europe. Electricity has now been rationed from 5 to 11 p.m. in Breda.

September 29 '44: No major news. It is not easy to do with no electricity at home.

September 30 '44: There is a lot of traffic of the German Army in our city, including a lot of Red Cross vehicles.

October 2 '44: The famous harbor city of Calais has fallen to the Allies. Russian and Rumanian troops made good progress, were able to cross the Danube River and are on Yugoslavian territory.
Jetje and I visited friends and we all had a nice walk in the forest.

October 3 '44: Our family and friends gathered around the radio tonight, lo and behold we had electric power all day!

The British warned the population of our province Zeeuws-Vlaanderen which is located on the North Sea and has a very low level, to move away further west because heavy bombing of that territory and dykes is expected soon which will flood a lot of land. In the village of Putten apparently three German officers were killed. The Germans retaliated: all men from 16 to 60 years old were arrested and taken to Germany, the rest of the population was told to move away and the village was completely destroyed.

October 4' 44: Apparently the Canadian Army has made progress from Antwerp and is now 35 km from Breda! The Americans are making progress near the "Siegfried line" by Achen. Polish patriots in Warsaw have, after a 63 day battle, capitulated because the Russian Army, although very close to them, did not lift one finger to help them (Years later I was told by Polish officers that the Russians did that on purpose because those Polish patriots would probably be anticommunists). In Yugoslavia the Russian and American troops are making good progress and the free Yugoslavia forces under General Tito are on their way to their capital: Belgrade. Many Greek islands have been abandoned by the Germans and are now occupied by the British and Greek patriots.

Sad news: last night an outpost of the Dutch underground forces in the woods just south of Breda was found by the Germans, then surrounded and hit with heavy machine gunfire. Several fighters were killed and the remaining ones were captured and taken to the S.S. Command post on Juliana-lane.

October 5 '44: Today is for me the saddest day of the war. As mentioned yesterday some underground fighters were arrested. One of them was my very close friend: Henk Hofman. Apparently early this morning they were taken outside the city, lined up and executed. Henk will be buried in 2 days but unfortunately Maarthen and I (we were the other two of the Triumvirate) cannot go to the funeral for fear of being arrested as underground fighters. What a sad day! And we are so close to being liberated. The British are already fighting past Baarle-Nassau, only 15 km. from us. The British and Canadians are making progress all around us.

The death of Henk hits all of us very hard. Today his body was released to the family. We went to see him and shared our sorrows with his parents and siblings. Henk's face showed the bullet hole which killed him, plus many bruises from beatings. As I said before we cannot go to the funeral but the girls are going and we will visit his grave as soon as it is safe.

A police inspector visited the Hofman family and told them that he was present when Henk was interrogated by the Germans. Apparently they asked him why he did what he did. Henk answered that he planned to join the British forces immediately after the liberation. The German then said: "You are a very brave man!"

October 10 '44: The main goal of the Allies is now to fully liberate the harbor of Antwerp, so they can much easier bring in troops and supplies. Secondly

199

the crossing of the Rhine River is crucial. In the East a large part of Greece has been liberated. Apparently just in time because the population was starving to death.

The situation of the Northern 2/3 of our country (North of the Rhine River) is dismal. There is almost no coal left which means very little electricity, gas and water. The food situation is bad and the Germans are taking a lot of food back East. Many men are being deported. The Germans are also planning when they withdraw to break the dykes which will flood a large part of the Netherlands. We are blessed to live south of the Rhine.

We received a letter from my sister Liesje, who works as a nurse in a hospital in Utrecht. She is very busy doing her work and is trying to "hang-in-there!"

October 12 '44: In Utrecht the Germans went door-to-door and arrested about 4000 men to work for the German Army. Five boys who had done some sabotage were arrested then pulled behind cars on the road and then executed. The "Green Police" carried this out.

In the liberated part in Holland in the South people are very happy, are eating much better than in years and are even playing sports: soccer, PSV-English team 10-2. Jetje and I went to Henk's grave for the first time. We met Frans Latour there who was visiting his mother's grave, who died recently. He told that a few months ago on her birthday, Henk was dancing with his mother.

The Russians are making good progress in Hungary and in the Baltics. Mr. Churchill and Mr. Eisenhower are in Moscow to talk with Mr. Stalin.

October 13 '44: Athens has been abandoned by the Germans. Piraeus, Athens's harbor has been liberated. In our province Zeeuws –Vlaanderen two towns were liberated.

There was a dramatic happening in Breda- 4 British fighters bombed a house, in which they had located the German general staff. Sadly they bombed the property next door which was a rest home for older people, called Bad-Warishofen. Tens of people were killed.

I was just in the neighborhood with Robje and a friend, not more than ½ mile away. The loud sounds of machine gunfire and bombs was overhelming. Many windows shattered. When the attack was over we went to have a look. I found my friend Maarthen who was as white as a sheet. He had watched the attack from about 100 yards.

We all chipped in to help whatever possible, which was very difficult with wounded people beneath the rubble. Late afternoon we found a lady under a large pile of material. There was also the danger of falling objects. In the morning Robje and I will return there to help as much as we can.

October 15 '44: We spent most of the day yesterday back at the rest home to clean rubble etc. The Public Works Department was now in charge and had their own people. However after sometime they needed volunteers, so we were called and then worked hard. A total of 26 people were killed.

Later on I spent time with Jetje's younger sister Cor to help her with school work. Our subject was Latin and fortunately I still remembered a lot from high school. Close to our home several homes were taken over by the Germans so we hope and pray that they will leave us alone. This morning the sugar factory on the edge of the city was attacked and bombed by the RAF.

Other news: the capital Riga in the Baltic's was liberated by the Russians and they are fighting inside Belgrade. Hungary which was the only German ally other than Japan and Italy has capitulated to the Russians. The Allies are making further progress in Zeeuws-Vlaaderen. Petsamo was the last big harbor for the Germans in the far North in Finland. The Russians just took Petsamo. The famous German Field-Marshall Rommel was wounded in July by an Allied air raid and died.

October 17 '44: Progress is being reported in Hungary, Belgrade and in Italy. Also within miles from us. A young German officer was moved into our house yesterday. He was very polite and made his bed perfectly. He is moving on today. Some people and bicycles are being confiscated by the

Germans. Again I am helping Corrie Blokhuis with Latin.

October 18 '44: Our German "friend" officer came back to spend the night. In Mammie's conversations with him he said that he is actually from Austria and not a strong Nazi-member. The Canadians are making further progress in Zeeuws-Vlaanderen. The Germans are gradually withdrawing from the Finish-Norwegian border.

We received a letter from Liesje who is working as a nurse in a large hospital in Utrecht, which is a medium sized city. She says that there is steady flow of hospital admissions of sick and wounded people. The doctors are exhausted and have to operate by flashlights. Food is getting scarce. She also says that the city is very quiet because thousands (mostly men) have been taken by the Germans to work on military installations.

October 19 '44: The Germans have put up big placards with the order for the population to bring in clothes, stipulating what you are allowed to keep: 3 pairs of shorts, sweater, one pair of shoes etc. "Bring in the rest." Marshall Stalin announced a large new offensive to begin soon to take Czecho-Slovakia. The Greek government has moved back into Athens. Hitler is calling all boys and men from 16 to 60 years old into the military.

October 22 '44: A new offensive has been started by the British North of Antwerp in the direction of Roosendaal and our city Breda. The British have made some progress around Arnhem and Nijmegen-Belgrade has now been completely liberated by the Russians and Marshall Tito's forces. The conference between Churchill, Eisenhower and Stalin has ended and Churchill is safely back home. We look forward to the details.

Good news from the Pacific: General MacArthur has successfully landed on Leyte, one of the main islands in the Philippines. He has established his headquarters there.

October 24 '44: The German artillery in the frontline is now only a few kilometers from our home. More Northwest from us in the city Den Bosch (the capital of our province short for 's-Hertogenbosch) several smaller towns have been liberated such as Osmalen , Berlicum and St. Michiels-Gestel and there is already fighting reported in the streets of Den Bosch. In East Prussia the Russian Army is making progress and several towns have been liberated.

Lithuania has almost been completely cleared of German forces. Progress is being made in North east Hungary. Finish troops are making progress in Finland.

In Albania, free Albanian forces have liberated another city (the harbor Valona). In Greece the British liberated another city. Mr. Churchill will outline his discussions with Stalin to the British people in 2 days in the House of Commons.

October 25 '44: A few more towns in our province have been liberated. The British are now within 3 miles from Tilburg (which is only 15 miles to our west) The Canadians are also progressing in our province. Northwest of Belgrade Tito's troops liberated 2 more cities. More cities have been liberated in Greece. In the Far East a large sea battle is taking place between the American and the Japanese fleets. The Japanese lost one aircraft carrier and two more were damaged. Six battleships and a few cruisers were also damaged. The Americans lost one light aircraft carrier.

OUR LIBERATION

November 7 '44: I did not write for two weeks but very much happened in this period. It appears that the Germans abruptly left and abandoned our city on October 28, including all their civil offices and bureau's etc.

In the morning of October 28, Robje and I called to the headquarters of our O.D. group (Our Dutch underground Army group to which we belonged most of the war). I have not been able to write about this and our activities because our activities were always secret. On October 28, we were sent to the frontlines to check out German firing positions which we then would pass on to the Allied forces by radio. We did not realize then how close the liberation was.

We traveled on our bikes. Our assignment took us first in the direction of Effen and Rijsbergen. The whole area was clear of Germans. Only one road was blocked by fallen trees and a German guard watching over the situation. On the way back at the edge of the Mastbosch (a forest just outside our city) we found 3 Germans pieces of artillery firing, which were reported. We progressed further when suddenly we ran into incoming fire. Allied grenades fell close to us. The grenades came close and we jumped into a dry ditch for protection.

I felt as if someone hit me in the left neck. It was bleeding pretty good and Robje pushed a piece of cloth on to the wound. We called for help but no one was around. Robje ran to the nearest house, with me following slower and keeping pressure on my neck to slow the bleeding. We were able to reach the house, owned by a family we vaguely knew and I was treated in the basement. We could not reach a doctor so they decided to transport me. Fortunately two men of the Red Cross came and bravely took me to the nearest big hospital risking their own lives.

The doctor told me that the shrapnel had not hit a major artery but only 1 to 2 inches deeper my spinal cord would have been cut. He was not able to remove the shrapnel.

I was taken home. My parents were shocked and my sister cried. Once resting on a nice mattress at home I thanked God for me being still alive.

The rest did not last long because in the early evening incoming fire started around our neighborhood. We spent most of the night in the cellar with the whole family. Our electricity gave up and there was trouble with the water lines. In the meantime the grenade fire kept coming.

Sunday October 29: was a very great day. Polish troops (the first Polish tank division, part of the British Army) entered our city. Suddenly we heard a machinegun firing close to our home in an eastward direction. We heard footsteps in our front yard and a strange language being spoken and through the small window of the cellar we saw a couple of strange looking soldiers ducking in our front yard behind the front wall. In spite of the danger we went upstairs, even myself in spite of still feeling weak from my injury. To our great enjoyment we saw the Polish soldiers. Also tanks were passing by our house: we were being liberated! What a sight!

A few Polish soldiers briefly entered our home. In the course of that day the whole city was being liberated and thousands of people came out of their homes to celebrate. Robje went immediately to our Underground Army Headquarters to check what we should do next. Many girls who fraternized with the Germans were caught and their heads shaved bald. That night we still spent in the cellar because of possible German incoming fire. Several cities in our province have also been liberated: Tilburg, Den Bosch, Roosendaal and Bergen-op-Zoom. The province to our west, Zeeland has also been liberated.

I am still mostly resting to gain my strength back; Guusje and Jetje came by for a visit. They were very concerned about me. It is nice to get so much attention, especially from ladies.

Robje came home briefly. He is now a military man in the open: he wears a helmet and a big belt with hand grenades. He wears an official armband indicating his rank and affiliation. The Polish artillery fires now regularly close to our home and the sound is earth-shattering. My friend Maarthen comes to visit briefly. He is now adjutant of one of the Western commanders and even drives a car.

We still have no electricity and water.

Allied troops by the hundreds are passing by. Nearby the Polish Army occupied a previous German home. They invited us for dinner. What a joy! Many languages went back and forth: Dutch, English, German and Polish and thus we communicated. We had a wonderful time and at the end we all received some cigarettes and a bar of chocolate. In addition they gave us a nice tin of cookies. One soldier told me that they had a Polish surgeon and he would pick me up the next morning at 10 a.m. to see him.

Fortunately I can now sit in bed and walk a short distance. We had several cases packed with our clothes so we could leave at a moment's notice. Now we can unpack and put our clothes back in the closets. The radio is now openly in the room. In the streets you saw Allied soldiers everywhere and the shops are selling some chocolates, tea and cigarettes, although in small quantities.

We have running water back! H a l l e l u j a h!

I visited today with Dr. Dobrecki, the Polish surgeon. We need an X-ray to determine the precise location of the shrapnel in my neck, but for that we need electricity, so he just re-bandaged the wound.

Two of my friends came over to visit and brought me some gifts; even George Ivanoff from our headquarters came to visit.

Several Jewish people who were hiding for several years came out in the open. In one case a mother had been hiding in the top of the house for two years, while the children downstairs had no clue that she was there.

Several Polish troops came to visit us; they tell us interesting stories, for instance that the Germans sometimes put landmines under dead bodies so that the person who comes to take care of the deceased, gets hits which an explosion.

November 7 '44: X-rays have been taken of my neck but Dr. Dobrecki said that even though he could see the shrapnel it would be better to wait with surgery so that my blood loss would be resolved and I would be in better shape. I have a nagging neck pain and shoulder pain but otherwise I am in fair to good condition. I have been visiting my headquarters but I cannot be of much help other than in the office. Therefore I signed up with the Civil Service as interpreter.

Practically our whole province has been liberated but

the poor people who live North of the Rhine River are still occupied by the enemy. When will they be free? Fortunately the access to Antwerp is now in Allied hands which will help enormously to bring supplies in. Greece is now completely liberated and the Russians are already fighting in the outskirts of Budapest.

This is the end of my diary covering the last few months leading up to our liberation and the liberation itself.

ADDENDUM III
HOW TO SAY A FINAL GOODBY
FROM THIS LIFE ON EARTH

My friend Jack Rider was a member of the U.S. Air Force and a Korean War Veteran. Early in 2013 he was diagnosed with a late stage lung cancer. Jack knew that he would not live much longer and that chemotherpy and radiation would only grant him a very short postponement of his death. He also knew that these treatments would have strong side effects and would make him suffer terribly. He chose to let nature take its course. He died July 3, 2013. Two months prior to his passing he wrote a poem. I was very privileged to get permission from Janet, Jack's wife, to publish this poem in my book. Here it is:

My Final Thoughts
God has called me home
Heaven's gates have swung wide
Jesus stands with open arms
And then I am at His side.

When God called me home
He said, "I need you here."
Oh, what peace and joy it is
To have Him so near.

213

Please have no sorrow
And there's no need to cry
'Cause Jesus tells me
"I'll see you by and by."

Please hug and love your family
And tell your friends you care
'C God wants all of you
To be with me up there.

Please pray for my loved ones
Every day and every night
And give them you assurance
That everything is all right.

Let Christ be your foundation
Let Him give you peace and love
And let Him embrace you
And you will fly on the wings of a dove.

There's no need
To say, "Goodby."
I'll meet you later
In the sky.

To God be the glory!

Amen

D. Jack Rider

I hope that my readers are as impressed with Jack's words as I am. It has touched me deeply and enhanced my Christian faith. I believe it to be one of the most beautiful, moving, relevant and powerful expressions of a Christian man's testimony I have ever come across. May it do the same for you, my readers.

Good-bye, Jack. I look forward to joining you in the not too distant future.

CLOSURE

I faced death four times to within hours or inches.

First, the firing squad when I was 16 to within 12 hours.

Second, I passed through several German military check points on my bike with a big block of dynamite. Had I been stopped I would have faced another firing squad.

Third, I moved out of my apartment in Amsterdam while being an underground Army member. The next morning the German Police came to the apartment to arrest me. Had I not left, my arrest would have resulted in execution.

Forth, while under fire on the frontline with my brother, I received a piece of shrapnel in my neck. It stopped one inch from cutting my spinal cord.

Why did this happen?

I believe that I had a job to do in His greater glory and I thank Him for it. I am still in the process of working for Him by treating elderly patients in their homes. All this is very humbling and what an honor it is to be a servent of the LORD!

Pictorial
Account

Political opponents of the German occupants are being rounded up.

Destruction by the German bombers of Rotterdam. May '40 in the first few days of the German invasion of the Netherlands, about 30 miles from my hometown.

Aan de Commandant te Utrecht.

De Nederlandsche Verdedigingsstelling aan de Grebbe is ingenomen! In de meerderheid zijnde Duitsche strijdkrachten zijn paraat, van het Oosten, Zuid-Westen en Zuiden onder gelijktijdigen inzet van sterkste Pantser-en Luchtstrijdkrachten (Bommenwerpers en Stuka's) de stad Utrecht in te vallen.

Hierdoor vorder ik den Commandant te Utrecht op, den doelloosen strijd op te geven en de stad over te geven om de stad zelf en de Inwoners het lot van Warschau te besparen.

Ik vorder U op, Uwe onvoorwaardelijke overgave te seinen (Frequenz 1102 kHz, Roepteeken: hol).

Anders zou ik tot mijn spijt gedwongen zijn de stad Utrecht als Vesting te beschouwen en den aanval onder inzet van alle militaire middelen te beginnen.

De verantwoording voor alle daaruit voortkommende gevolgen ligt uitsluitend bij U.

De Duitsche Opperbevelhebber.

14 Mei 1940

May 14 '40 The German order to the Dutch forces to stop any resistance.

BULLETIN no. 3.

Eerste pagina van het eerste nummer
van het 'Bulletin' - en een van de ma-
kers: N. G. Voûte

First publication of Vrij Nederland, *a resistance
newspaper. At the bottom: "Our country will
never become a German province" – "long live our
fatherland" – "long live the Royal Family"*

Nazi arrest of Dutch citizens.

Notorious Buchenwald concentration camp.

Mauthausen concentration camp.

Heden bereikte ons het droevige bericht uit Duitschland van het overlijden onzer beide geliefde Zoons

KURT en RUDI,

in den leeftijd van 29 en 22 jaar.

JACOB HAIMANN.
AMELIE HAIMANN—
GOLDSCHMIDT.
Courbetstraat 21.

Heden ontvingen wij bericht, dat in Duitschland op 25 Juni is overleden onze innig geliefde Zoon, Broeder en Zwager

AB. LOPES DE LEAÓ LAGUNA,

in den leeftijd van 24 jaar.
Namens de familie:
B. LOPES DE LEAÓ
LAGUNA.
Verzoeke geen bezoek.
Smaragdstraat 25 I Z.

Met diep leedwezen geven wij kennis, dat onze innig geliefde eenige Zoon

PAUL JACOBUS LEO,

in den ouderdom van 27 jaar, 25 Juni in Duitschland is overleden.

I. HEIMANS JR.
J. B. HEIMANS—
VAN GELDER.
Amsterdam, 1 Juli 1941.
Watteaustraat 5.
Liever geen rouwbeklag.

Wij ontvingen heden het droeve bericht, dat onze geliefde Zoon, Broeder en Kleinzoon

ARNOLD HEILBUT,

in den leeftijd van 18 jaar, in Duitschland is overleden.
Amsterdam, 2 Juli 1941.
Z. Amstellaan 89.
H. M. HEILBUT.
F. HEILBUT—CARO
en familie.

Dutch newspaper announcements of family members' death by execution in German captivity (ages 18 to 29).

Gasoline shortage leads to primitive transportation.

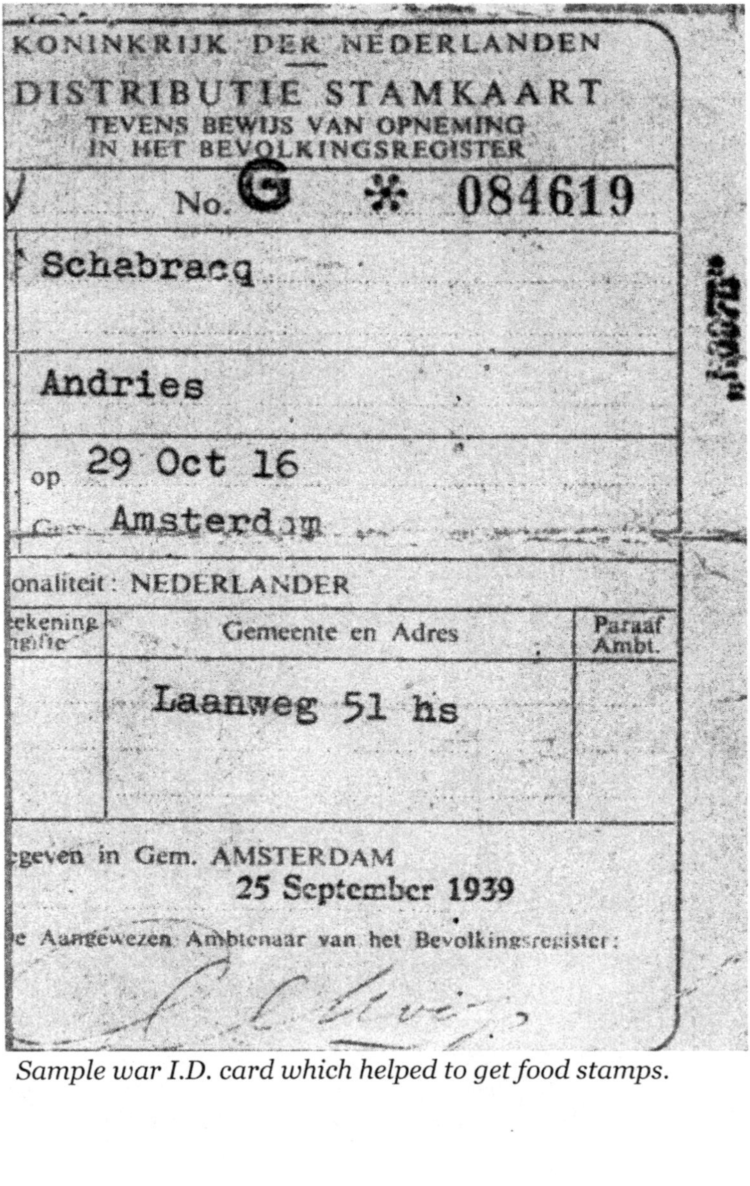

KONINKRIJK DER NEDERLANDEN

DISTRIBUTIE STAMKAART

TEVENS BEWIJS VAN OPNEMING
IN HET BEVOLKINGSREGISTER

No. G ✳ 084619

Schabracq

Andries

op 29 Oct 16

Ge.. Amsterdam

..onaliteit : NEDERLANDER

..ekening ..gifte		Gemeente en Adres	Paraaf Ambt.
		Laanweg 51 hs	

..geven in Gem. AMSTERDAM
25 September 1939

..e Aangewezen Ambtenaar van het Bevolkingsregister :

Sample war I.D. card which helped to get food stamps.

The Royal Air Force strikes the Philips factory in Eindhoven Dec. 6 '42. The allied bombers killed about 30,000 Dutch people during WWII.

Top: "Restricted area for Jews"
Middle: "Jewish quarter"
Bottom: "No Jews allowed"

Mr. Eichmann, mostly responsible for the Jewish "resolution"

Jews transported to concentration camps in railroad cars.

Two heroes who bravely and secretly kept communicating with London from occupied Holland and who were finally captured by the German military. Their final letters to their family showed a powerful pride in the work they did for their country without any hesitation and knowing that they would be executed—there were thousands like them. The final word on the brothers grave says: "God's will prevails".

The infamous winter of '44-'45 was probably the worst in Dutch history. The South was liberated, which meant that I was free and able to join the British Army for the rest of the war, but the Northern three-fifths of the country remained occupied by the Germans until May '45. Many starved to death.

A woman's story in Feb '45: "I went on my bike, carrying an expensive table service planning to change it for food. The farmers did not want my gift. The best they could do was to give me a sandwich. They looked at me sadly that they did not have any other foods to give me. I returned home with my service and without food."

Germany's last special weapons: The V1 (unmanned)

The V2 (above). It traveled a few hundred miles, then crashed down and exploded. The V2 (also unmanned) shot straight up at an angle like a missile than came straight down and exploded. I can still remember these weapons coming over us. The scary part was when the engine stopped and you were waiting for the crash-landing.

One of Hitler's last pictures (above). One brutal weapon of the German occupation was to punish any act by the resistance with the execution of hostages. At one occasion a 13-year-old boy was executed! A total of three thousand Dutch people were killed by execution during WWII.

"Oom" (uncle) Hannes made special trips to Amsterdam to resue Jewish children who were close to being transported to German concentration camps.

The liberators begin to come down in Holland in the summer of '44.

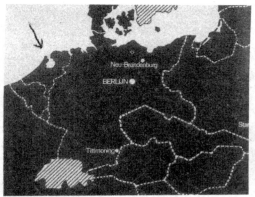

Map of Western Europe (see arrow for Holland)

Indonesian prisoners of the Japanese shortly after their liberation.

Prince Bernhard (Princess Juliana's husband) returned to Holland after the liberation. He was the official commander of the Dutch Underground Army during the last few months of the war. He was my "boss".

Aboard a Dutch U-boat.

The Dutch people helped the Americans wherever possible.

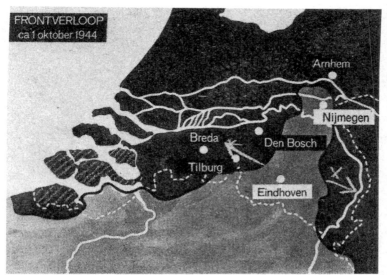

Map of Southern Holland with my hometown Breda.

Sample of our welcome (when I was in the British Army in the end of '44) "long live the Tommy", when we liberated other parts of Holland.

Food droppings in the last stages of the hunger winter.

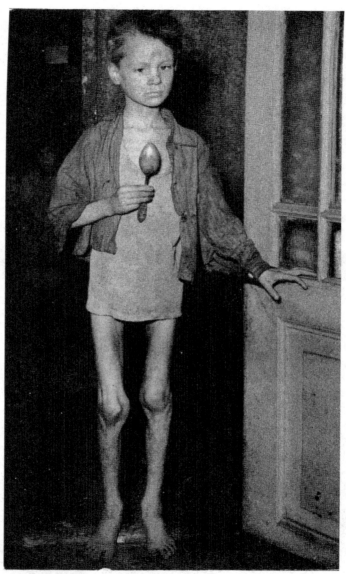
Holland's hunger winter '44-'45.

CPSIA information can be obtained
at www.ICGtesting.com
Printed in the USA
FSOW04n0214080616
21176FS